PALMISTRY

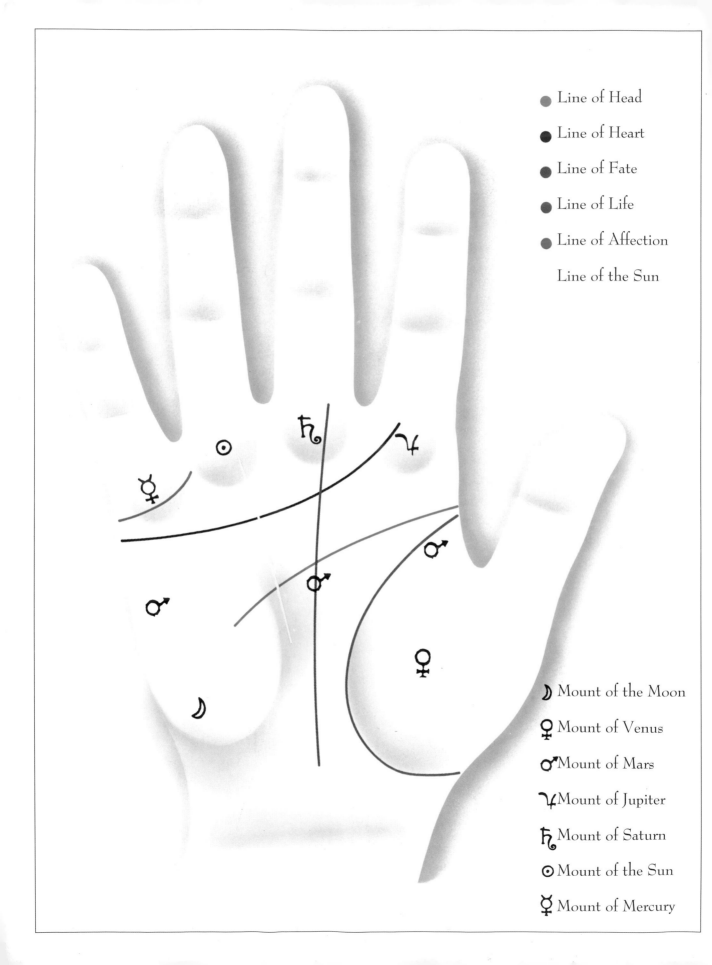

- Line of Head
- Line of Heart
- Line of Fate
- Line of Life
- Line of Affection
- Line of the Sun

☽ Mount of the Moon
♀ Mount of Venus
♂ Mount of Mars
♃ Mount of Jupiter
♄ Mount of Saturn
☉ Mount of the Sun
☿ Mount of Mercury

PALMISTRY

How to Chart the Lines of Your Destiny

ROZ LEVINE

A Fireside Book
Published by Simon & Schuster Inc.
New York   London   Toronto   Sydney   Tokyo   Singapore

I dedicate this book to my daughter, Rebecca.

FIRESIDE
Simon & Schuster Building
Rockerfeller Center
1230 Avenue of the Americas
New York, New York 10020

FIRESIDE and colophon are registered trademarks of Simon
and Schuster Inc.

10 9 8 7 6

Library of Congress Cataloging-in-Publication Data
Levine, Roz
    Palmistry : how to chart the lines of your destiny / Roz
Levine.
    p. cm.
    ISBN 0-671-78501-X
    1. Palmistry. I. Title.
    BF92.L48 1993
    133.6–dc20   92-334
                                                           CIP

AN EDDISON · SADD EDITION
Edited, designed and produced by
Eddison Sadd Editions Limited
St Chad's Court, 146B King's Cross Road
London WC1X 9DH

Phototypeset in Bernhard Roman by SX Composing Ltd,
Rayleigh, England.
Origination by Columbia Offset, Singapore.
Printed by Dai Nippon, Hong Kong.

Contents

Introduction   6

CHAPTER ONE
THE HAND AS A CANVAS   8

The Language of Hands   10
The Right and Left Hands   12
Significance of Shape   13
Reading the Fingers   14
Comparing Fingers   16
The Landscape of Mounts   17
The Three Worlds   18
Nail Shapes   19

CHAPTER TWO
CAREER, AMBITION AND MONEY   20

How Motivated Are You?   22
Job Satisfaction   24
Leadership Skills   26
Signs of Success   28
Money Matters   30
The Entrepreneur   32
Direction and Development   34
Family and Career   36
The Time Factor   38
Timing Major Events   40
Career Changes and Breaks   42
Sample Reading   44
Common Questions   46

CHAPTER THREE
TALENT AND POTENTIAL   48

The Artistic Hand   50
The Performer   52
A Way With Words   54
The Inventive Hand   56
Designs on Structure   58
Assessing Academic Ability   60

The Outdoor Type   62
The Scientific Hand   64
Healers and Helpers   66
Psychic and Intuitive Signs   68
Sample Reading   70
Common Questions   72

CHAPTER FOUR
LOVE AND RELATIONSHIPS   74

Love and Happiness   76
The Fickle Heart   78
The Passionate Lover   80
The Hands and Compatibility   82
Soul Mates   84
Will You Have Children?   86
More Than One Love?   88
A Law Unto Themselves   90
The Broken Heart   92
Sample Reading   94
Common Questions   96

CHAPTER FIVE
HEALTH MATTERS   98

The Healthy Hand   100
You Are What You Eat   102
Heart and Back Problems   104
Minor Ailments   106
All in the Mind   108
Depression and Anxiety   110
Pressure and Trauma   112
The Road to Recovery   114
Necessary Tensions   116
Accidents, Addiction and Life-style   118
Sample Reading   120
Common Questions   122

Afterword   124
Index   125
Acknowledgements   128

INTRODUCTION

Look down at your hands. You may not realize it but every aspect of your being is reflected there: your talents, character, strengths, weaknesses are all displayed, as well as all major events still to come in your life. All you need to know about yourself is literally at your fingertips. And, once you have read this book, all you want to know about other people will be there on *their* palms — ready for you to read with your new-found skills.

Through the centuries there have been doubts and suspicions about palmistry — this most harmless of divining arts — but now it is recognized as a valuable means of self-discovery and an accurate method of reading a person's character and destiny. Some people have dismissed the lines on a palm as merely creases, but the fact is there are many more lines present than the movement of your hands and fingers could cause.

What Palmistry Can Tell Us

Many people automatically assume that palmistry is just about the lines on the hands. But the hand as a whole — the overall shape, including the fingers, nails and joints — is just as important because it reveals character. Together, the shape and size of the palm and the lines marked on it show habits, actions and past, present and future events.

The hands are a barometer of health. They can show when one's health is below par before an actual illness takes hold and manifests in the rest of the body, thus allowing preventative measures to be taken. The Line of Life is particularly relevant to health matters, but many other lines and features also have much to say. People often mistakenly believe that the Line of Life is the sole indicator of longevity. Although this line reveals much about health, the Line of Fate too is relevant to life expectancy and other future influences.

We all want to be loved. Love is the nucleus of all our emotions and we all need to give and receive it. The complexities of human relationships, however, make affairs of the heart the most difficult aspect of life for many of us. Your hands can show the sort of relationships you have experienced and those you may anticipate. They can reveal how an existing partnership or love affair is likely to develop. Children, or potential children, are also shown on the lines of the palm, but do not always refer to actual physical offspring. These lines can signify the birth of ideas, such as when two people come together in a creative meeting of minds.

Reading Another Person's Hands

To study palmistry, all you need is this book and some hands to explore. When carrying out a reading for someone else, however, there are a few guide-lines to follow. Firstly, make sure that you are both comfortably seated and as relaxed as possible. Sit beside each other, so that the hands are upright when you are examining them, like most of the examples illustrated in this book. Good lighting is essential. A lamp that shines on to the hands and does not glare into your faces is best. Some people have very fine lines, so a magnifying glass is often useful. And bear in mind that a *modus operandi* or a sequential way of going about your reading is a good approach.

You will find that some people are a little shy about having their hands touched and held, especially by someone of the opposite sex. You *will* need to touch the hand in the initial part of your reading to find out how flexible and springy it is, but thereafter in such instances, it can be a good idea to use a pencil to track and point out the various lines on the hand. Never insist on reading the palms of someone who clearly does not want to be scrutinized in this way. And remember that when reading another's hands, it is important to relate what you see there in an objective way — never a judgemental way. We all differ in our attitudes to our life-styles after all.

How to Use this Book

This book covers many aspects of character and life's events that are familiar to most of us. You will find much that links in with your own experiences, or those of people you know, and every page has something new and interesting for you to learn. I have devised *Palmistry* in a special way for those who have never studied the art before. It is also a useful guide for those who have attempted to learn how to read hands but have found other books written on this most fascinating subject difficult to understand. The most challenging aspect of learning palmistry can be in identifying the different lines on the palm, so I have created a colour key to enable the novice to locate the lines with ease and confidence. From my experiences as a palmist, I have found that there are certain questions that I am asked time and time again. Each chapter deals with the lines of an important area of life, like work, talent, love and health. At the end of each chapter, there is a special question-and-answer section, which covers many of the key issues in our lives. Like the colour code, it will help to teach you in a quick and informative way.

To prepare yourself to learn about the lines on the palm, I suggest that you read Chapter One before going any further. This deals with the shape, size and appearance of the hands and fingers, important aspects that reveal the basic personality. You will then be able to read whichever section of the book interests you most, but be sure to work through the whole book, as each part includes something different that may apply to your life.

For those of you who have already learned a little about palmistry, this book will further your knowledge readily; and if you have never approached the subject before, the following pages will open up a new world for you, deepening your understanding of yourself and others.

Chapter One

THE HAND AS A CANVAS

Your unique and individual character is mirrored on your hands. Imagine the hands as a canvas, the lines and features upon them as the paint that colours all the hues and tones of your personality and predispositions. The picture, however, is likely to change in time.

You can alter the lines upon your palm. With will and effort, you can be the designer and artist creating the picture of your own destiny. Your metaphorical box of paints is likely to include some colours you never thought of using before. If we link the idea of colour to ways of thinking and being, we may realize that we have so often been using greys and flat, dull tones, whilst forgetting to dip into the brighter, positive shades of hope and love. When these colours are unused, they become dry and cracked, but remain in your paintbox. So use them to colour your life in the best way you can.

The following pages will reveal how the shape of the hands, fingers and the contours of the palm constitute the framework of your personality.

THE LANGUAGE OF HANDS

When you are trying to discover the personality of someone you have just met or do not know, how often do you find yourself looking at his or her hands? You may not even do this consciously, but the way in which people use their hands will be telling you much about the personality of the owners.

In many ways, the hands can reveal more about someone than the face, especially when it comes to first impressions. We can change our facial expressions, 'put on a brave face', smile with just our mouth but not with our eyes, etc. Make-up can make people look very different and many people succumb to the plastic surgeon's scalpel. Hands, however, have a language of their own that is less easy to manipulate. When people are carefully controlling their facial and verbal expressions, their hands are often telling quite a different story. Gesticulations can therefore be very revealing. Think of how the hands are used to demonstrate so many feelings: drumming fingers in impatience, making fists in anger and pointing the forefinger in aggression or accusation. Biting, picking or clicking the nails, cracking the knuckles and other fidgety habits usually suggest a nervous disposition or a habit stemming from childhood that is difficult to break. Effeminate men often affect a limp wrist and women tend to have looser and more flexible wrists than men. Look at the hands of tiny babies: even at this early stage in life, individual gesticulation patterns are established.

In business, we set great store by the handshake: if it is firm, we interpret it as a good, decisive sign, while a weak handshake is taken as an indication of a vacillating, unassertive nature. Remember, however, that a firm handshake can be faked. There are far more subtle ways to find out the way another person is thinking. Supposing you are discussing a business arrangement with someone and notice that the thumbs are held inwards, towards the palm. This suggests that the other person is not revealing feelings of annoyance and may also be secretive. A more positive sign is rubbing the fingertips together, especially those of the thumb and the little finger, which occurs when trying to generate the flow of ideas. Ring-twisting shows convoluted thinking. Placing the ring finger under the middle one can mean that financial issues are not being openly revealed.

Hand gestures are also used to insult others. In some countries it is rude to point the index and middle fingers up at someone, forming the 'V' sign. The origins of this insult are interesting. When the longbow was used in battles, these two fingers drew the bow, and soldiers had them cut off when they were taken prisoner. For this reason, the fingers were often pointed at the enemy in a victorious, jeering gesture.

The fingers rings are worn upon can also be revealing. In old paintings of important people, rings tend to be worn on the index finger, the finger of power and ambition. Gay people often adorn their little fingers with a ring. A ring chosen to fit the middle finger can link with a slight psychological quirk or problem. Making a fist is obviously aggressive and reveals tension. Rubbing hands together usually signals pleasant anticipation. As you can see, there are many ways in which our hands express what we think or feel.

Above. The open hand with fingers that splay out means that the owner is open to life's experiences. Such a hand often brings a harmonious disposition and a love of life, but originality may be lacking.

Above. These fingers are held together indicating that this person may not want his or her palm to be read. Such a palm brings confidence and a dislike of opposition.

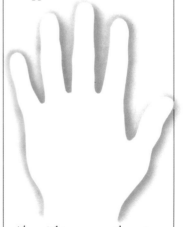

Above. This curve on the outer edge of the palm is known as the Creative Curve. Here, on the lower edge, it denotes physical energy.

Above. When found higher up on the edge of the palm, as shown here, the Creative Curve, or Curve of Strength, can increase the owner's strength and sometimes activates ideas. It does not, however, create physical energy.

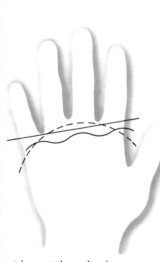

Above. When the fingers are set uniformly into the palm, it can denote a balanced personality, someone who may not have to struggle to achieve desired goals. When the fingers are set unevenly into the hand, however, it can mean that life will be more unpredictable.

Open and Closed Hands

When you look at hands placed upon a flat surface, it is interesting to note how the owner holds them. Some people naturally allow their fingers to splay open; this literally shows that the overall personality is also likely to be open and that the person is receptive to having his or her hands examined. If the fingers are naturally held close together, the opposite applies and the owner may not be as keen to be scrutinized. Open hands often have spaces between the fingers at their roots where they join onto the palm. You can see the spaces more easily if the fingers are held together and the hand is held up to the light. This means that the person not only has an open nature, but is also generous and friendly, often gregarious, sometimes a little vulnerable and will usually be open to new ideas and experiences. If the fingers bend back easily away from the palm under slight pressure, then the above attributes will be marked and there will also be adaptability.

If there are no spaces between the fingers, the owner may be rather good at holding on to what he or she has, in all senses. On the closed hand if the fingers do not yield to slight pressure when bent away from the palm, but naturally turn inwards towards the palm, it reveals a personality that is far less spontaneous, gregarious and willing to reach out for new experiences than the open-handed type. Inflexible fingers reveal a tendency to resist change: the owner will wish to hang on to things and people that are familiar, adhering to crystallized patterns of existence. Such a person will always need a certain amount of time to adjust to any new phase in life.

Hand Size

The size of the hands can also be extremely revealing. It does not necessarily follow that a large person will have big hands, or that a small person will have little ones. To judge whether hands are big or small, they must be considered in relation to overall body size. Big hands generally belong to people who are good at handling detailed and even intricate activities. A brain surgeon would be likely to have such hands. Small-handed people do not generally take to things that require detailed thought or intricate actions as they tend to apply themselves to matters in hand in a quick and sometimes more intuitive way. The natural impatience of people with small hands is exacerbated if the fingers are short. If the nails are naturally short as well, then the lack of patience could be a real problem.

Small hands often belong to people who are good at organizing and handling things on a large scale. Very dynamic, high achievers with the ability to direct others will usually have hands that are small in relation to their overall body size. Small hands tend to be warm to the touch, whilst long, big, bony hands are often cool. In some ways, this can be seen as a reflection of the two temperaments. Small, neat hands found on a person with a large, tall body can denote great dexterity in handling many activities and can create good co-ordination.

As a rule, owners of broad hands need a feeling of physical freedom and space (see The Outdoor Type, pages 62-63). Those with narrow palms, however, are usually happy with much more indoor, static lifestyles, and can be good at jobs that require a lot of desk work.

THE RIGHT AND LEFT HANDS

Are you right-handed or left-handed? This is the first thing you need to ask when you examine someone's hands. The two hands have a different significance. Physically, they usually vary too, in the shape of the fingers and especially in the lines, although some people's right and left hands are virtually the same.

Always begin a reading by asking the person

tells us a lot about a person's feelings of confidence and adequacy, this person would have suffered from a lack of confidence, especially early in life, but will grow into far more self-certainty. Note also that the left hand shows a small and weak-looking ring finger, whilst the right hand shows the finger as stronger, no longer rather dwarfed by the middle finger. The owner of such

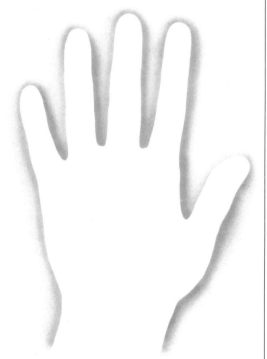

Look carefully at the left hand and decide how it differs from the right hand. Often the hands can be very different. This right hand has a more even and balanced look than the left hand in that the middle finger is not too long and the index and ring fingers are stronger. As the left hand shows basic tendencies and the right shows how the personality will change, it follows that, in this case, there may be certain fundamental imbalances that would eventually even out.

whose hands you are looking at whether he or she is right-handed or left-handed. Some people are ambidextrous in many ways, in which case it will be the hand used for writing that shall be regarded as the 'right' hand. The 'left' hand shows the basic personality and predispositions as well as past and current events. The 'right' hand shows how the basic personality has changed or is likely to develop and indicates future events. When you are reading the hands of a left-handed person, you will regard the right hand as the basic one, reflecting the present and past events, and the left as the hand linked with the future.

The two hands illustrated (above) have very different fingers. The index finger is much shorter on the left hand than on the right. As this finger

hands would have problems with being positive and discovering creative energies; but as time goes by these qualities will develop.

There are no hard-and-fast rules about how long our fingers should be as our hands are all unique. Usually, however, the index and ring fingers are about the same length, their tips ending halfway up the top section or phalange of the middle finger; the little finger should end at the crease of the ring finger's top phalange. As you read on, you will learn about the lines of the palm and their meanings and see just how different lines can be on each hand. Whenever there is a marked difference, you will know that the owner of the hands has changed, or will adapt, a great deal in the course of his or her lifetime.

Significance of shape

There are six basic hand shapes and each reveals a great deal about the personality of the owner. It can be easy to assess the shape of the hands from a distance, so once you understand their meanings you will find yourself looking at the hands of people wherever you go.

The hand shapes explained here are archetypal, in that they are very defined types. As you look at more hands, you will find some that obviously belong to one category or another and others that are a mixture of shapes, such as a square palm with spatulate fingers. Sometimes fingers differ from each other on the same hand. If each finger is different, there will be great versatility, sometimes too much, rendering focus and defined direction difficult to achieve.

When you look at the shapes of hands and fingers, do take into account the age of the subject. Older peoples' hands often have distorted bones due to arthritic or rheumatic tendencies, which can become stiffer as the owner ages.

The philosophic hand is a slightly more unusual shape than the five other basic types. It is long, bony and angular with knotty fingers. People with such hands are often interested in religious, literary or occult matters, or other areas that benefit from serious or analytical thinking. They are difficult for others to understand and can be withdrawn. If the finger joints are very knotty, an aptitude for deep, analytical thought will be amplified.

The elementary hand often has few lines on its palm. When this is the case, the rather basic, instinctive nature will be even more simplistic. Pointed and conic hands often have many lines upon them, but if they do not, then the nervous tendencies associated with these hands shall be more earthed and the owner will be able to handle life more calmly. Square hands can benefit from a rather lined palm, in that the need for conformity is given some leeway and freedom. The owner of a very lined spatulate hand can be over-active and find relaxation difficult.

Above. The elementary hand looks meaty and strong and is not very flexible. Pay attention to the thumb: if it is very short and rigid, basic needs and passions will be amplified and not easily controlled.

Above. The square hand is likely to belong to someone practical, logical, solid and serious. Such types often choose methodical professions, but as imagination can be lacking, they are not usually drawn to creative careers.

Above. The pointed hand is often beautiful to behold: slight, delicate and probably smooth-skinned. This is the hand of a dreamer, an idealistic, other-worldly type who can sometimes be impractical and not very strong.

Above. The conic hand is tapered and round, often with long fingers. It denotes an artistic temperament: someone who is emotional and very sensitive, especially to form, colour and sound.

Above. The philosophic hand is characterized by its knotty joints. It reveals someone who thinks very deeply. The knottier the joints, the more prone the owner is likely to be to analytical thought.

Above. The spatulate hand has wide fingertips, broader at the ends. The owner will be active, imaginative, original and often unconventional. Spatulate-handed people can also be impulsive and impatient.

READING THE FINGERS

In palmistry, each finger has its own characteristic, which can be very revealing about personality. Each finger is named after a planet. The illustration (below left) shows the relevant planetary symbol on each finger. The first, or index finger, is called Jupiter ♃. It is associated with self-confidence, ambition, a positive attitude to life and sometimes with religion. The second, or middle finger, is called Saturn ♄ and is the finger of responsibility, seriousness and balance. It serves as a dividing line between our external personality and our inner world. The ring, or third finger is called the Sun ☉ and corresponds with our creative feelings and urges, though not necessarily in the artistic sense. This finger can also reveal one's capacity for happiness. The little finger is called Mercury ☿. It is linked to mental ability and communicative skills and, to some extent, attitudes towards sexual matters.

Finger Types

There are four main finger shapes or types of finger. Square fingers reveal a practical, conventional, sensible and well-organized disposition. If the fingertips are uniformly square, there will be a strong sense of order, a realistic approach to life and a love of punctuality.

People with pointed fingers are extremely sensitive, often quite impractical and can be rather difficult for more realistic and worldly types to understand. If all the fingers are pointed and their tips are long, there will be a dreamy, unrealistic and often over-idealistic attitude. Beauty will be important and reality will often be difficult to come to terms with.

Conic, or round fingers, belong to quick, intuitive people. Such types can be impressionable and therefore vulnerable. Sympathetic, spontaneous and easily moved, conic-fingered folk can sometimes be inconsistent in their emotional responses to others.

Spatulate fingers belong to active, original, energetic people who possess enterprise and a sense of adventure. The enthusiasm generated by a person with spatulate fingers can affect other people positively.

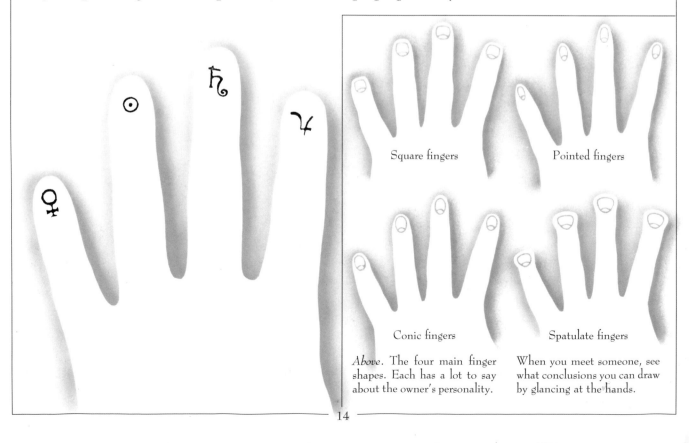

Square fingers

Pointed fingers

Conic fingers

Spatulate fingers

Above. The four main finger shapes. Each has a lot to say about the owner's personality.

When you meet someone, see what conclusions you can draw by glancing at the hands.

Thumbs

There are two main types of thumb: the supple-jointed and the firm-jointed. The more supple the thumb, the easier it will bend outwards and backwards away from the hand. When supple and flexible it donates a person with a flexible disposition and a broad mind who can sometimes be unconventional. This person will tend not to be too opinionated and will therefore be receptive to new ideas. The owner of such will hate discord and always try to avoid aggressive situations. There can be a generous nature, exhibited not only in material ways, but also in a generosity of spirit. Humanitarian attitudes can be another attribute of the flexible-thumbed type, as can frankness and honesty. If the thumb is very flexible, an impulsive response to life is likely. The only negative aspect of this type of personality is that there can also be a tendency to promise more than can be delivered in an effort to please others, which may need to be held in check sometimes to avoid disappointing people and appearing unreliable.

The stiff, firm thumb shows a resistant character: the less it yields and bends backwards under pressure, the more resilient and stubborn will be the nature of its owner, who is not as friendly and forthcoming as the flexible type. People with stiff thumbs can have strong opinions and be very determined. They usually need time to consider everything as they lack spontaneity. If the thumb is rigid and held very close to the hand, an antagonistic, argumentative nature is indicated, sometimes with dogmatic, inflexible ideas and opinions and a lack of tolerance. This type of person will need patient, understanding friends. With encouragement, even those with the most inflexible thumbs can be helped to 'loosen up'. Such a change in attitude can sometimes, in time, be reflected in a slight change in the thumb itself.

The top phalange of the thumb relates to the will; the lower section relates to reason and logic. The longest of the two will have the greater influence in the personality. Flexibility is, once again, an excellent sign in the case of either or both phalanges. If the lower section feels looser and more flexible than the top, the owner will be better at adapting to circumstances. Reasoning power will be used to adjust to situations and the need to adapt to people will be a secondary consideration. If this is reversed, with a more flexible top section, overt wilfulness will be modified.

When the centre of the thumb, between the top and middle areas, has a defined 'waist', or noticeably thinner part, it reveals a propensity for tact and diplomacy in putting things across to others. This is generally an excellent sign, bringing qualities that are useful in so many areas of life. If the thumb has no waist whatsoever, it reveals a certain lack of tact but the ability to use argument and reasoning power to make a point. People with straight thumbs can sometimes be rather pedantic, with a determination to be in the right, whatever issue is under discussion. This is, however, a stubborn, rather than aggressive trait.

The shorter the thumb — in relation to the hand as a whole — the less reasoning ability there will generally be. If the thumb is very short, it can indicate a definite lack of control over the passions and emotions. This is especially applicable to stiff, unyielding thumbs. A long thumb, conversely, reveals a more diplomatic personality.

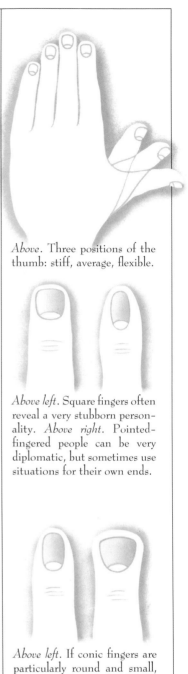

Above. Three positions of the thumb: stiff, average, flexible.

Above left. Square fingers often reveal a very stubborn personality. *Above right.* Pointed-fingered people can be very diplomatic, but sometimes use situations for their own ends.

Above left. If conic fingers are particularly round and small, there may be a lack of will-power. *Above right.* Spatulate-fingered people are usually tactile, often in an artistic way.

Above. A short, clubbed thumb, can reveal a highly instinctive, sometimes violent nature.

COMPARING FINGERS

Many fingers are not totally straight, but lean towards a neighbouring finger to the left or right. This can reveal further aspects of the personality.

Straight fingers, which do not lean to left or right (see top right), indicate that the quality associated with each one will be clearly defined in the personality. The owner of a straight Finger of Jupiter ♃, for example, will have much self-confidence (see Reading the Fingers, pages 14-15).

The Finger of Mercury ☿ is concerned with communication. If it leans away from the other fingers (see middle right), the owner is likely to have, at least, an independent way of thinking. Sometimes it can bring awkwardness and even an uncooperative attitude. This finger is also linked closely to sexuality; if it is very isolated from the others, the owner may tend to find some difficulty in self-expression in close interactions, which can aggravate existing conflicts. The straighter the Finger of Mercury, the more straightforward will be the thinking. When it bends inwards towards the Finger of the Sun ☉ (see bottom left), the owner may be inclined not always to tell the truth and may, in a child-like way, tell white lies or even 'grey' ones.

If the Finger of the Sun ☉ leans towards the Finger of Saturn ♄, this indicates a conflict between responsibility and seriousness and the need for light-heartedness and happiness. Sometimes, and especially if the Finger of the Sun is short in relation to the Finger of Saturn, there can even be guilt feelings, which can cast a shadow over the sunnier side of the personality. At worst, there can be a depressive tendency, but other factors reduce or amplify such a trait (see Depression and Anxiety, pages 110-111).

The Finger of Jupiter ♃ leaning towards its neighbour, Saturn ♄ (see bottom right), means that there will be a strong desire to acquire possessions. This may not be greed, but linked to actual needs that create anxiety over material concerns. This can sometimes mean that the owner of such a palm is untrustworthy to a certain extent. Such a tendency will not be marked unless other factors reinforce it, such as a Finger of Mercury ☿ bending inwards towards the Finger of the Sun ☉. The way in which the hand is held will help to clarify whether it is need or greed that promotes acquisitiveness. If the hand tends to curl forward into itself, the urge to have and to hold on to things will be strong. If the hand is of the open sort, however, especially when there are spaces between the fingers at their roots, then any greediness will not be strongly felt; although there may be an acquisitive tendency, there will be some generosity too. When reading someone's palm, remember that the straighter the fingers the better, although the tendencies revealed by fingers that lean to the left or right may not always be pronounced or constitute a real problem.

Above. Here the fingers are straight, not leaning towards one another.

Above. Held separately from the rest of the hand, the Finger of Mercury ☿ shows a tendency to think and speak in a fractious way. The Finger of the Sun ☉ is weak, leaning on Saturn ♄. Positive feelings may be outweighed by heavier influences in this case.

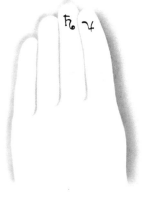

Above. The Finger of Jupiter ♃ leans towards its neighbour, Saturn ♄, indicating some acquisitiveness, perhaps born out of insecurity.

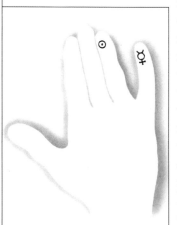

Above. A tendency to lie can be shown in the way the Finger of Mercury ☿ leans towards the Finger of the Sun ☉. People with hands like this tend not to get over things easily.

The landscape of mounts

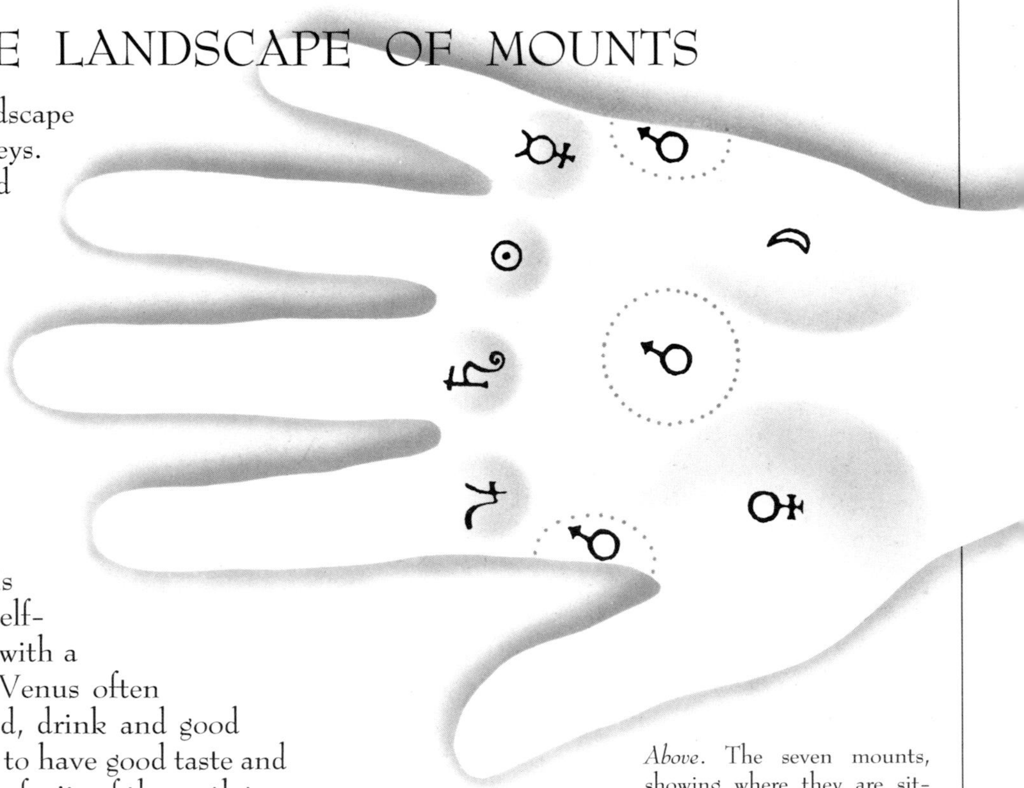

The palm is like a landscape covered in hills and valleys. The highest areas are called mounts and each one, like the fingers, is named after a planet.

The Mount of Venus ♀ is the fleshy area below the thumb. The higher this mount, the more capacity for love there will be. If the hand as a whole is very fleshy and stubby then this trait can degenerate into self-gratifying passion. People with a reasonably full Mount of Venus often have a love of nature, food, drink and good times generally. They tend to have good taste and love pleasing others with the fruits of the earth to generate warmth and pleasure. A flat Mount of Venus can indicate that the affections may function more on the mental or spiritual planes than the physical.

Above. The seven mounts, showing where they are situated on the palm: Venus ♀ Moon ☽ Mars ♂ Sun ☉ Mercury ☿ Jupiter ♃ Saturn ♄.

The Mount of the Moon ☽ is linked to the imagination, idealism, romance and travel. If it is very developed, the owner will be capable of sympathy, as this mount strongly connects the individual to other people's needs. Sometimes a very full mount can indicate an over-emotional attitude, which means that the owner is unable to see reason easily. Sometimes a full Mount of the Moon corresponds with strong religious views and practices.

When the Mount of Jupiter ♃ is developed, there will be a need to be in charge of one's own affairs as much as possible.

A very developed Mount of Saturn ♄ shows a rather heavy and even sombre nature, with a tendency to take things too seriously. A flat or virtually non-existent Mount of Saturn denotes someone with a frivolous nature who never takes anything too seriously.

A large Mount of the Sun ☉ denotes a need to be in the limelight. It is generally considered better to have a large rather than small Mount of the Sun: although it can indicate a rather bumptious disposition, at heart there can be love, joy, warmth, loyalty and largess.

The Mount of Mercury ☿, when developed, brings eloquence, mental dexterity and plenty of ideas. If it is very full, there shall be an abundance of mental energy.

There are three Mounts of Mars ♂. If the mount nearest the thumb is the most developed, it will increase energies, sometimes to the point of pugilism. The central mount should feel bouncy showing that the inner energies and powers of resistance are generating well. If this area is soft and malleable, energies can be below par. When the mount at the outer edge of the hand is developed, it can correspond to a restless inner state or mental aggression.

On some palms, two mounts will merge. The creative Mount of the Sun ☉ merging with the innovative Mount of Mercury ☿, for example, can inspire creative ideas.

THE THREE WORLDS

The palm can be divided into three areas, which correspond with the three main aspects of being. This division has been known as the 'three worlds' of the hand since ancient times. The longest section discloses a great deal about the fundamental disposition and likely response to life. The three sections of the fingers are also very revealing.

The Palm's Three Sections

The upper area of the palm is linked to the the mind, spirit and one's ideals and aspirations. This section includes the fingers and the area where they join the palm. When is the longest, intellectual and spiritual interests will be the major motivating forces in life.

The middle area of the hand starts where the fingers join the palm and ends at the lower sections of the Mounts of Mars ♂. Connected with the practical, 'here-and-now' world, it reveals an ability to be effective in practical ways.

The lowest section of the palm begins below the Mounts of Mars ♂ and runs to the bottom of the hand. It is associated with our basic desires and urges. If this area is the longest, our instincts will tend to be our main motivating factors. Physical energies are usually in good supply.

Reading the Phalanges

The fingers are divided by their joints into three sections, called phalanges. Like the three areas of the hand, the top phalange is linked to the mind and spirit, the middle with practical matters and the lowest with our basic needs and urges. If the characteristics of each finger (see pages 14-15) are taken into consideration when examining the phalanges, further fascinating aspects of the personality can be discovered.

The Meanings of the Longest Phalanges

The Finger of Jupiter ♃

Top: pride, dignity and a sometimes contemplative nature.
Middle: ambition and business ability.
Bottom: a desire to rule; a lack of refinement.

The Finger of Saturn ♄

Top: studious and superstitious tendencies.
Middle: a talent for investigative work.
Bottom: financial aptitude; materialism.

The Finger of the Sun ☉

Top: poetic ability.
Middle: strong business interests.
Bottom: bad or ostentatious tastes.

The Finger of Mercury ☿

Top: good communicative ability.
Middle: a talent for practical communications.
Bottom: abilities in business and commerce.

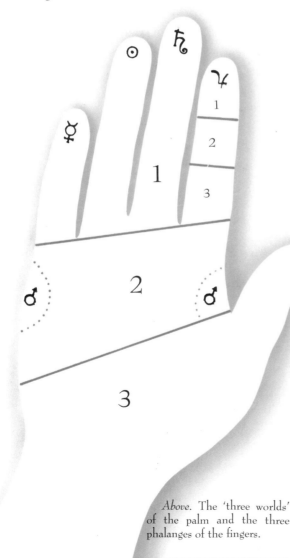

Above. The 'three worlds' of the palm and the three phalanges of the fingers.

Nail shapes

The finger-nails, like the fingers, reveal a lot about personality. They are also a valuable means of spotting health problems, which will be revealed in Chapter Five. There are many different nail shapes, which are classified into basic types. It is unusual to find a hand with the same type of nail on every finger, but when they are all uniform, the characteristic associated with the nail type will be a strong factor in the personality. Different nail types on one hand reveal a personality that has a variety of influences working on it.

When the nails are square, there may be problems with self-control, especially if the nails are also very pink. Feelings of anger or frustration will be difficult to keep in check. The owner of paler nails, however, will tend not to have such a quickly impassioned response.

Sometimes square nails are naturally extremely short. They are often found on the hands of people who lack diplomatic skills and are unable to see things from anyone else's point of view. This type will often doggedly stick to some petty idea or belief. Trying to argue a point with them or suggest a different and perhaps more reasonable way of seeing things is useless. They are stubborn, with a limited perspective and a very short fuse. Sometimes they can be unreasonably jealous in sexual matters.

Tact and diplomacy will also be absent when naturally short nails are found on hands with short upper phalanges. This type of person is likely to be impatient, to respond instinctively to life and others, to be very critical and to jump to conclusions. If the hand as a whole is short, stubby and thickset, a bad temper is likely. This will be even more marked if the palm is red or has very red lines upon it. Sometimes this type also has a defensive attitude. If, however, the finger-nails are short, but the top phalanges of the fingers are long, the above traits will be modified, and an element of thought and reason will serve to lend some control and tact.

In effect, the breadth of the nails is a channel of energy. Wide nails will therefore tend to generate more energy than narrow nails.

Above. Square nails indicate impatience, but there will usually be an ability to control a short temper and to apply reason to irritating situations.

Above. Sometimes square nails are also naturally very short. This often indicates a narrow attitude and lack of reason.

Above. Broad nails, when not short, literally reveal a broad-minded attitude. On spatulate, flexible hands, understanding and tolerance for the ideas of others will be marked.

Above. Almond-shaped nails indicate a refined, sensitive, diplomatic nature. In extreme cases, there may be a tendency to embellish or not reveal the whole truth.

Above. Long, almond-shaped nails may look attractive, but they can sometimes correspond to certain physical weakness or malfunction.

Above. Very narrow nails suggest a lack of strength, a sensitive body and active nervous system, especially if the palm is very lined.

Above. Claw-like nails can be likened to the talons of a bird. They often reveal a dominating and superior attitude. It is not unusual to find them on the hands of older people who have difficult, tenacious dispositions.

Chapter Two

CAREER, AMBITION AND MONEY

Not everybody is consumed by burning ambition, but most of us would like to achieve something in life. The following pages will show you the lines and features of the hand that can reveal ambitious urges and tell you whether or not they are likely to be realized.

Many people find themselves working in occupations that are unsuitable. The hand, fingers and the lines on the palm can show you the sort of work that is best for you. We are more likely to do something well if we are not having to go against the grain of our natural abilities.

We live in times of enormous world-wide upheavals — political, economic and technological — that affect us all. For some of us, they may bring about a shift of gears, or a break in career. How we respond to such changes, and the opportunities they bring, will show on our palms. We often fear change, but it is not always as cata-strophic as we anticipate.

Money matters to most of us. How we acquire it and our attitudes towards it — generosity or meanness for example — is revealed in certain lines and marks on the palm and the hand as a whole.

How motivated are you?

Motivation is often revealed by the Line of Fate. Sometimes known as the Line of Destiny, it is usually located in the middle of the palm running up towards the Finger of Saturn ♄ (see below). The Line of Fate can begin anywhere on the palm, ranging from the bottom of the hand close to the wrist, or higher up.

The Line of Fate reflects our sense of direction and purpose and is likely to be well defined on the palm of a well-motivated person. Most people do have some sort of Line of Fate, but if this is non-existent, it does not necessarily mean there will be a lack of motivation. People without this line can achieve a lot in life but will tend to 'go their own way', often refusing to conform. Their ability to realize a wider range of possibilities will help them to choose the course of action that is most appealing to them. They can therefore be well motivated in a very independent and individual way.

The illustration (right) shows a Line of Fate rising from the base of the palm and running directly up the hand to terminate beneath the Finger of Saturn ♄. It has no breaks and its course does not waver or weaken anywhere. Note how close it is at its beginning to the 'bracelets' or rascettes on the wrist. Such a line is likely to belong to a person who is extremely well motivated and there are other factors that compound this. Look at the thumbs (see page 15). If they are strong and determined, this is likely to be reflected in the personality. Examine the length of the fingers in relation to one another. A confident Finger of Jupiter ♃ and a positive Finger of the Sun ☉ will reinforce a strong Line of Fate and motivation will come naturally. Any branches rising from the Line of Fate will help the owner to achieve whatever his or her sights are set upon. These lines are very helpful influences that always indicate a significant increase in motivated attitudes and actions.

The Mount of Saturn ♄ is also linked to motivation. If it is higher and more developed than the other mounts, however, motivation shall still be forthcoming, but can be accompanied by a feeling of being burdened or trapped by the urge to achieve. Such a narrow focus can create limitation in other areas of life.

When the Line of Fate begins higher up on the hand, the owner is unlikely to feel a strong sense of purpose until he or she is of an age when the line begins to be defined. Time, as revealed on the hands, is explained on pages 38 to 41.

It is also important to examine both palms. Sometimes the left hand has no clear Line of Fate, whilst the right hand can be quite different with the line clearly defined. This tells you that the early part of life did not, or does not, feel charged with motivation or an urge to achieve, but that there shall eventually be more defined goals. When the right and left hands differ greatly in this respect, remember there is likely to be a big

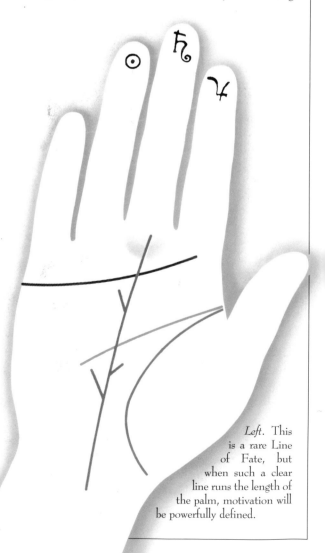

Left. This is a rare Line of Fate, but when such a clear line runs the length of the palm, motivation will be powerfully defined.

Above. Motivation, effort and ambitious actions are shown on this palm. A successful life is likely.

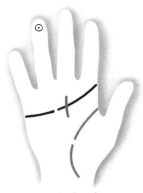

Above. Born lucky, but not very motivated, and with no sense of real personal achievement until towards later life.

Above. A very motivated hand, shown in the strong Line of Fate, a Line of Sun and a fork rising from the Line of Fate.

difference between early and later life and that a lot of adjustments will have to occur before a defined path in life can be pursued.

A person with a Line of Fate on the right hand only can sometimes have more choice in creating his or her career and future. Whatever predisposed talents there are may eventually emerge with a sense of purpose and motivation, although perhaps not till later in life. The late twenties often correspond with a time of defining goals.

If the Line of Fate is heavily etched onto both palms, it can show a well-motivated person; but he or she may be so strongly tied to destiny that there may be less opportunity to exercise choice about life's direction.

The Line of Life can also reveal a lot about a person's motivating forces. If it has a full, curved sweep towards the middle of the palm, it tells of an urge to get out and experience life in a full way and therefore could help to galvanize motivation.

The illustration (above left) shows a strong Line of Fate and a Line of Sun rising from a point just above an upward branch on the Line of Fate, indicating feelings of well-being and positive influences that may benefit finances too. Note also a line rising from the beginning of the Line of Life, veering towards a point between the Fingers of Jupiter ♃ and Saturn ♄. This is the so-called Line of Ambition. As it is angled slightly towards the 'serious' Finger of Saturn, ambitions will be taken seriously. This line stops at the Line of Heart suggesting that ambitions can sometimes be, or feel to be, blocked by emotional issues.

A powerful Line of Sun can be seen branching from the Line of Life and terminating below the Finger of the Sun ☉ (above middle). Note that the Line of Fate is very short. A person with such a strong Line of Sun could be 'born lucky' and realize success and probably prosperity. However, this does not necessarily mean happiness. If everything falls into one's lap with little effort, motivation could be lacking and there will be no sense of achievement. The Line of Fate begins very high on the hand, indicating that a feeling of accomplishment will be achieved later in life.

A Line of Fate forks towards the Finger of Jupiter ♃ (above right), indicating a powerful urge to be in control, certainly of one's own affairs and perhaps those of other people. This fork corresponds with a Line of Sun beginning at the same juncture on the Line of Fate, travelling towards the Finger of the Sun. This means that motivation will be marked and there may be rather ruthless tendencies.

Take into consideration the general tone of the hand. If it is soft, there will not be much impetus, even with a strong Line of Fate. We all need a certain amount of internal pressure to promote the energy necessary to move forward in life. Remember that some of us are born with motivation, some of us acquire it, while others are content with what life brings.

	Line of Affection		Line of Heart
	Line of Fate		Line of Life
	Line of Head		Line of the Sun

JOB SATISFACTION

How many people are truly happy with what they do to earn a living? The shape of a person's hands and fingers, and the Line of Fate, can reveal what sort of work he or she will be happiest doing.

Job satisfaction is also important to people not in paid employment. A busy mother bringing up a family can have as well-defined a Line of Fate as a business executive if she feels well-directed and satisfied with her life. Her work may not be regarded as a career, but it is nevertheless her job, so her attitude towards what she does will be reflected on her palm in the same way as a conventional career would.

A square-handed person will be methodical and will therefore enjoy an occupation that requires organization and a predictable routine. This will be especially so if the Line of Head is not sloping but lies straight across the palm, showing a logical mind. Square-handed people tend to deal with things in practical, realistic terms, and can really enjoy occupations that a more imaginative person would find excruciatingly boring.

Spatulate-handed types need variety, change and the opportunity to use their originality. If they were cooped up in a small, claustrophobic environment doing a repetitive task, they would feel enormous tension. These people need space and freedom to achieve their best.

Elementary types are not usually found in employment that taxes the intellect. This does not mean they are stupid, but that they are geared towards mainly earthy activities, such as building roads and cities, farming and cultivating the land. Civilization depends upon the strength of elementary hands to perform such manual tasks, so this type should not be undervalued.

Conic-handed people find most satisfaction in work that is creative or linked to the arts. They tend to be sensitive to the environment.

Those people with pointed hands will not enjoy

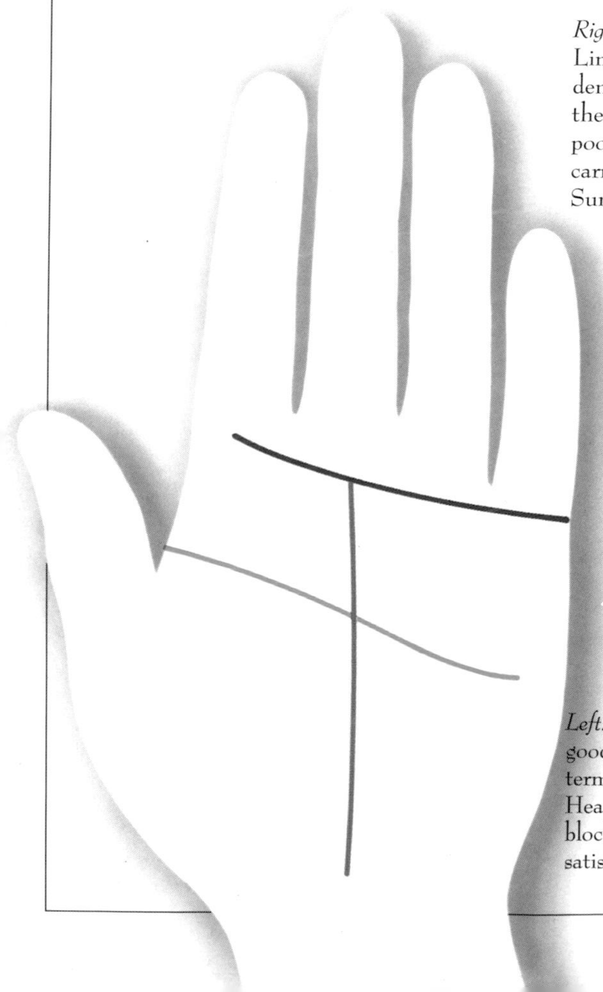

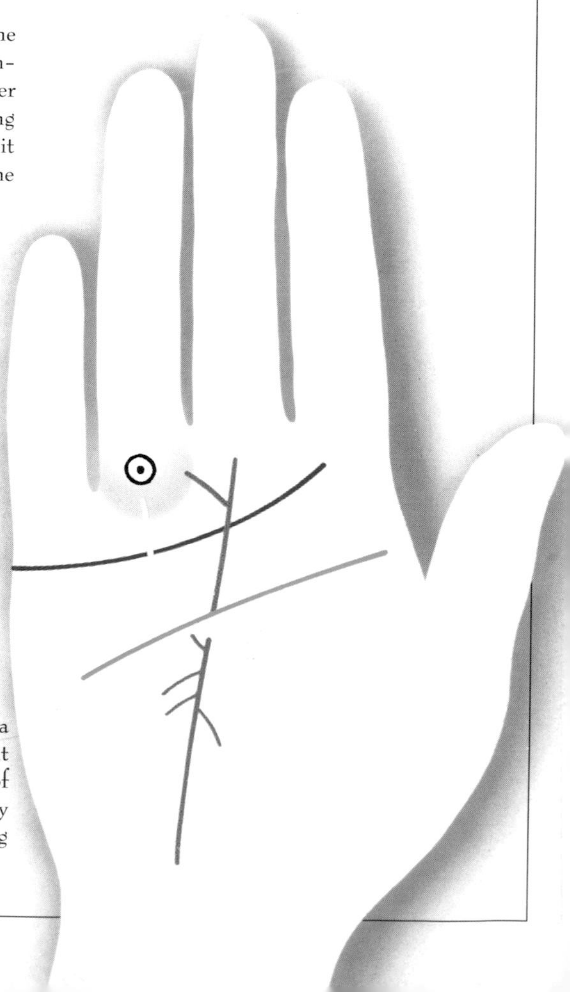

Right. Lines drooping from the Line of Fate indicate despondency. The line stops under the Line of Head meaning poor judgement. Happily, it carries on, and the Line of the Sun comes into effect.

Left. The Line of Fate shows a good sense of direction until it terminates under the Line of Heart. Unhappiness literally blocks the way to realizing satisfaction.

physically-tiring work. Their constitution can be rather delicate and their whole being can suffer if circumstances force them to work in any harsh or demanding conditions.

People with 'philosophic' hands – thin hands with knotty and exceptionally long fingers – need to use their ability to analyse and can work well by themselves. They are aesthetic and, like those with conic or pointed hands, are sensitive to the working environment and other people and need harmonious conditions. Peace and quiet may be sought to allow for concentrated mental effort.

Mixed hands – a combination of hand and finger shapes – show the ability to apply oneself in various ways. Such people are very adaptable, but so much so that choosing a satisfactory occupation can be difficult. They can be talented in more than one area, a 'jack of all trades', knowing a little about a lot of subjects. They may need to cultivate whichever talent predominates (see Chapter Three).

The Line of Fate is most beneficial when finely etched onto the palm. A broad line, cut deeply into the hand, together with a high Mount of Saturn ♄, can mean that the owner has little choice about which career to pursue. Although a deeply defined Line of Fate means that a career can be successful, the owner of such may feel bound to his or her work and derive little satisfaction from it. A weak or absent Line of the Sun will compound this. Sometimes a broad and smudgy looking Line of Fate can suggest overwork.

Emotional factors can help or hinder every aspect of life. If one's heart is not in one's work, or if there is an unhappy marriage or relationship to contend with outside the workplace, it can affect the way we view our working lives and our professional performance. An emotional issue that thwarts and undermines life's direction is revealed by a Line of Fate terminating beneath the Line of Heart (see page 24, left). If the line resumes its course, however, positive changes will lead to more satisfaction eventually.

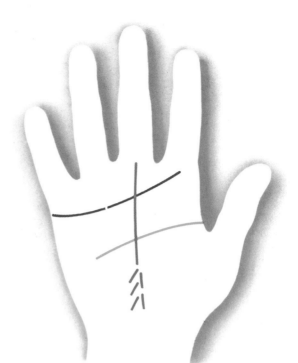

Above. A Line of Fate with many fits and starts shows a very unsettled career and life direction till around the early thirties. It then becomes well-directed, with a corresponding Line of the Sun ensuring lasting satisfaction.

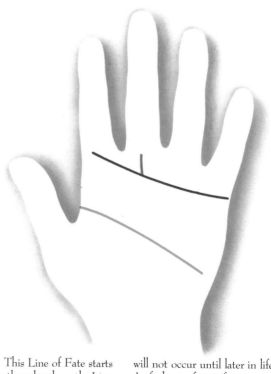

Above. This Line of Fate starts high up the palm above the Line of Heart. It shows that a sense of direction for this person will not occur until later in life. A feeling of satisfaction will come eventually, but it is unlikely ever to be very profound.

Line of Affection		Line of Heart	
Line of Fate		Line of Life	
Line of Head		Line of the Sun	

LEADERSHIP SKILLS

Above. A firm thumb with a full pad on the top phalange is a sign of leadership. If the thumb has a 'waist' it will increase tact and diplomacy.

Above. A Line of Fate begins near the outer edge of the hand, showing a career linked with the public. It starts independently, literally telling of a determined start in life.

Some people are born to be leaders; others to be followers. Several features on the hand can show leadership qualities. The first and most important thing to examine is the overall strength of the hand: if it looks strong, able and capable, the owner could possess leadership qualities, for to be a leader one needs to be physically resilient and have stamina.

The shape of the hand can also reveal a talent for leading others. A square hand reveals the ability to organize; a spatulate hand usually belongs to energetic and adventurous types; a combination of both is also a good hand shape for a leader. A leader's hand is likely to be small, which shows ability to tackle things on a large scale.

The fingers and their lengths are also relevant here, as are the mounts. A leader is likely to have a strong and perhaps longish Finger of Jupiter ♃. A developed Mount of Jupiter increases incentive and, if it is really prominent, shows an urge to 'lord it' over others and a tendency to be very proud. Such a person will always prefer to lead rather than follow.

The Line of Fate is also important when gauging leadership ability (see above). Here the line runs straight up towards the Finger of Saturn ♄ ending on its mount and sends a line shooting off towards the Mount of Jupiter ♃. This shows that the work or main line of interest will bring with it the power to direct one's own interests and to have authority over others as well. Leadership skills may have been acquired in this case, as opposed to being an inherent driving force in the personality. When the Line of Fate sends a branch up to Jupiter, always look carefully at the Finger of Mercury ☿: if it is long there will be great powers of persuasion and the ability to project ideas well. Such attributes will enhance leadership skills and are particularly useful

Above. Leaders often have an inflexible thumb, which promotes determination and stubbornness. A developed Mount of Mars ♂ shows aggressive purposefulness.

——————	*Line of Affection*
——————	*Line of Fate*
——————	*Line of Head*
——————	*Line of Heart*
——————	*Line of Life*
	Line of the Sun

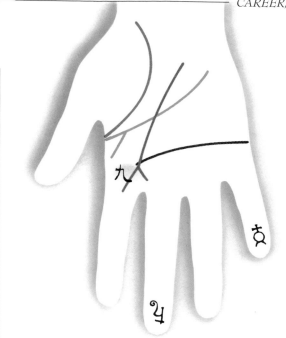

Above. The Line of Head rises towards Jupiter ♃, revealing that highly ambitious thinking and ideas are likely; when this is combined with an errant Line of Fate, the owner may be a rather ruthless individual who finds it nigh on impossible to take direction from anyone. Such a person may have an all-encompassing urge to be in charge not born of any higher motives or ideals, but a driving force to control.

in careers that involve oratory, such as politics, religious leadership or teaching. If the Line of Heart ends beneath the Mount of Saturn ♄, the owner may be rather insensitive towards other people. The urge to lead, which is not tempered by compassion, could create difficulties for the leader as well as for the follower.

Somebody who wants, above all else, to be in charge may have a Line of Fate that veers away from the usual path of the line to travel directly towards the Mount of Jupiter ♃ (see above). Saturn ♄, the area towards which the line usually travels, is the planet linked to a sense of balance, so when the Line of Fate is found 'off the beaten track', a decided imbalance will be indicated, which in its extreme could manifest as megalomania. The Finger of Mercury ☿ and the Line of Heart help to define the level of communicative ability and emotional capacity, which could help to temper a hand like this.

On a square hand, a Line of Fate with a branch towards the Mount of Jupiter ♃ can be an indicator of success in professions where there is

scope for ambition. If a Line of the Sun is also present, the owner will be assured of a fulfilling career in financial terms. This line will also bring a positive attitude to life, which could benefit both the individual and others in many ways.

The urge to lead can grow from a desire to help other people. Showing others the way to go, or what to do, can be a means of assisting or guiding them in idealistic or altruistic ways. As most people tend to be followers, people with leadership skills are essential to society. If a political or social set-up were suddenly to lose the guiding influence of its leader, it would not be long until someone else came to the fore.

The illustration (below) shows a Line of Fate that begins to be strong and well-motivated fairly early on in life. It makes its way, straight and true, towards the Mount of Saturn ♄, its natural place of termination. When it moves over the Line of Head, another Line of Fate comes into effect. This new line begins to travel towards the Mount of Jupiter ♃; though this certainly tells of an ambitious attitude, it will have evolved and been worked for.

Below. There is a second Line of Fate on this palm, starting on the Line of Head. An additional Line of Fate like this one will always strengthen the destiny and career of the owner; and when it pulls towards Jupiter, it will reveal someone who will definitely develop leadership skills.

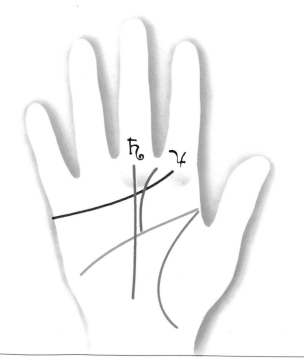

SIGNS OF SUCCESS

We all have successes and failures. Success usually means achieving one's goals and is relative to individual life-styles, expectations and values. A gardener, for example, may be highly successful in growing the best tomatoes and flowers for miles around, but to a very ambitious business person, success may only be measured in terms of money and power.

Success, in broad terms, will be found when there is a good Line of the Sun, and a clear, well-defined Line of Fate, which links us to our destiny and purpose and brings a sense of achievement.

Like everything else, success can come and go. Some people realize a blaze of success before the onset of maturity. A rock star, for example, may leap into the charts at an early age with a really successful recording, but then luck may run out and the fleeting star becomes a one-hit wonder. A hand showing short-term public success is likely to have a Line of Fate rising from the Mount of the Moon ☽ that will look especially clear at its beginning. The Mount of the Moon is linked to others, or the public, in various ways; people with such palms will therefore find that their destiny is greatly influenced by the capriciousness of changing public trends and tastes. This is especially so if the Line of Fate breaks up after a good beginning, becoming disconnected and fractured after it has risen from the Mount of the Moon. The owner of such a hand would be well advised to try to find another string to attach to

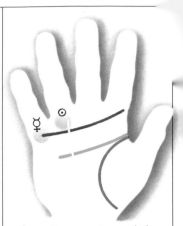

Above. A strong Line of the Sun, but no Line of Fate. Things may come easily but a sense of achievement may be lacking.

Above. Thin, delicate and pointed, this is a sensitive, dreamy and perhaps psychic hand. There is a good Line of the Sun, but as the hand is narrow with a hollow palm, the hypersensitive nature will negate its benefits.

Below. Wavy, uncertain, vacillating Lines of Fate and the Sun eventually move towards successful changes.

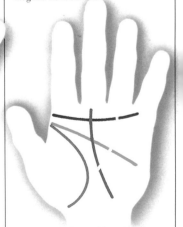

Above. Good Lines of Fate and the Sun; the latter ending with a star. This mark tells of great things: success, fame and fortune. It could, however, mean forfeiting a private life.

Above. A balanced hand, where the Line of the Sun emanates from the Line of Life, indicating a happy and successful life.

the bow of his or her destiny, particularly if the Line of the Sun is broken anywhere.

If the Lines of Fate and the Sun are wavy to begin with (see page 28, bottom left), the owner may not find a real niche, or realize success till around the mid-thirties (see pages 38-41 to find out about the hands and time). Then the Lines of Fate and the Sun begin reaching up from the Line of Head, showing that direction, positive, fruitful effort and thinking respectively begin simultaneously to work together well. A line branches from the Line of Head towards the Finger of Mercury ☿, indicating that thinking can be inspired, especially in ways of making money through communications. This branch can be linked to business and commerce and is often found on the palms of those who think a lot about financial matters. Mercury also links with travel and movement, so this palm shows that positive things happened via constructive interactions, probably in a new place, or through new methods of communication. A strong Finger of the Sun ☉ helps to promote bold and positive actions.

Some people just seem to be born lucky, geared to do well in life from the very first breath. They may not have any extraordinary gifts or talent, but possess a magical and magnetic quality called charisma. Charismatic people often have a defined Mount and Finger of the Sun ☉. But if success and achievement come about easily, it is essential to develop new interests or hobbies to prevent boredom setting in and to create fresh challenges. It is fine to rest happily on the laurels of success without letting one's life dissolve into negative complacency.

When you see a thin, pointed, sensitive hand that nevertheless has a good Line of the Sun, it means that the owner is likely to have a bright and sunny disposition, but will live in a fantasy world. Such hands belong to dreamers who are often extremely idealistic. They do not care too much about success in wordly terms, content with what is found within the realms of their imagination. If such a palm has a defined hollow area in its centre, then, sadly, even a strong Line of the Sun will not be felt in a very positive way. A hollow palm can negate, to varying degrees, other potentially good influences.

When the Line of Head slopes downwards on the palm, it shows imagination. Someone who has already realized the benefits of a successful life will be helped by such a line, as it will help him or her to find other areas of challenge or some goal yet to be achieved, through being in touch with a creative way of thinking.

Some people are more afraid of success than failure. They may have the potential to do great things, but are faint-hearted or lack confidence. Such a person might have a good, clear Line of the Sun and a sloping, creative Line of Head, but if a significant portion of the Lines of Life and Head is tied, this individual may hide natural talents and opt instead for the quiet life.

There are so many reasons why some people 'make it' and others do not. Bear in mind that most things of lasting value take time and effort.

Line of Affection	Line of Heart
Line of Fate	Line of Life
Line of Head	Line of the Sun

Below. A Line of the Sun is shown here, together with another, subsidiary line, which rises from the inside of the Line of Life, close to the base of the thumb. This area is linked to Mars ♂, the god of war. Here you would expect to find financial trouble, due to possible jealousy and interference as this line cuts through the Line of the Sun.

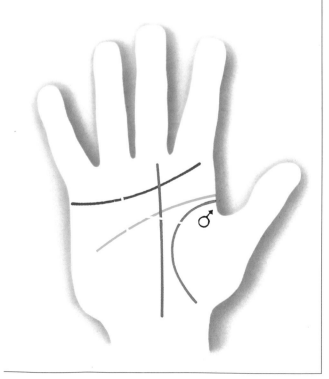

MONEY MATTERS

Left. Two branches rising from the Line of the Sun may belong to someone who will not only realize wealth, but who will also somehow revel in recognition. One branch veers towards Mercury ☿, showing an ability to use communications to further financial goals. This can be a generally positive line but is often especially useful in matters relating to business. The branch moving up towards Saturn ♄ reveals a balanced and sensible attitude, which will enable the owner to handle resources in a responsible manner with probable long-term benefit.

The most important thing in life for most people is love. The next is money. For some, however, money is the main concern. Security can be a state of mind, but for most of us security means that material needs are met so we can enjoy life and the freedom that financial security can bring. The hand, and the lines upon it, can reveal a great deal about money matters, can show our attitude to the material side of life and any aptitude for making – or losing – money.

The Line of the Sun is linked to success so it can be especially relevant to financial matters. This line is not present on every hand, but its absence does not necessarily mean that the owner will be unsuccessful with money. A financially successful person with no Line of the Sun is likely to have a defined Line of Fate. As the Line of the Sun is concerned not only with money matters but also with creative feelings and inner satisfaction or happiness, a person without this line who is able to make money easily may not feel a sense of contentment or indeed happiness. If the Line of the Sun is absent, this does not have to be a permanent state of affairs, for very often a person can only feel relaxed enough to get into the

creative side of his or her being when the material side of existence is taken care of and secured. So do not assume that someone without a Line of the Sun will always be unhappy and discontented.

Even the most materially successful person will experience difficult phases and have to respond to challenges. Special marks on certain lines can affect money matters. Small lines rising from the

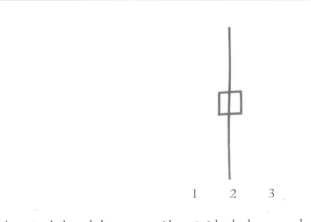

Above. Little lines helping or hindering the Line of the Sun. Rising lines are always a good indication but drooping lines are less positive.

Above. 1. Islands always reveal a time of difficulty. 2. Squares protect. 3. Crossbars signify obstacles and challenges.

Line of the Sun towards the top of the hand show helpful influences, which will boost financial affairs and can help promote material aims and ambitions. Little lines drooping from the Line of the Sun show slightly negative influences: not financial crisis but a need to be determined and focused in money matters. Sometimes they suggest slight despondency, or flagging; the owner may have a lot to contend with that is temporarily diffusing the desired goal.

When an island is found on the Line of the Sun, it indicates a time of trouble. This may not be serious, just rather bothersome and likely to involve other people: getting into hot water for not paying a parking fine or tax bill on time is the kind of thing that might happen.

A square appearing on the Line of Fate is a sign of protection. If there are difficulties linked to work and money matters, the square helps to ensure a safe passage through problematic times.

Crossbars on the Line of the Sun show obstacles. These can correspond to delays, frustrations and thwarting conditions affecting finances. Like the ones mentioned above, however, these marks are not to be viewed with too much trepidation as they are usually only short-lived influences.

A cross on the Mount of the Sun ☉ (see top right) is not a good sign. Crosses anywhere on the hand usually reveal some sort of problem to be dealt with, although there are some exceptions (which will be explained later). On the Line of the Sun crosses show that financial matters will be temporarily awkward, but if a cross is found on the Mount of the Sun itself, the mean-

ing is more ominous. Make sure you identify this cross correctly: it should be free-standing or at the end of the Line of the Sun, as opposed to a cross made up of other lines. When a cross is found, there is a strong possibility that the owner will experience at least some disappointment relating to money, and at worst financial disaster. The Line of Fate helps to tell you how serious things may be: if it is clear and strong with no breaks or fragmentation, then financial matters will be more readily and smoothly sorted out in troubled times.

The general shape of the hand and fingers can also be revealing when it comes to money matters. If the fingers of Jupiter ♃ and the Sun ☉ are the same length, there may well be an ability to make money, but there will also be a rather reckless attitude that sometimes leads to gambling, or to taking chances that are foolhardy and ill-considered. If there are wide spaces between the fingers at their base, then money could – quite literally – fall through the fingers like sand. A flat Mount of Saturn ♄ adds irresponsibility.

Square-handed people tend to be more prudent than those with spatulate or conic hands and fingers. If full, the Mounts of Venus ♀ and the Sun ☉ will reveal a love of spending money on beautiful things, and tastes may be rather ostentatious. If the Mount of Saturn ♄ is full but the Mount of the Sun ☉ is flat, and the hands are stiff and unyielding with no spaces between the fingers, there could be a Scrooge-like attitude towards money; and though it may not be in short supply, the owner would not feel rich, even when a good Line of the Sun is present.

Above. A cross on the Mount of the Sun ☉ indicates that great care must be taken in all matters relating to finances. There may be tricky situations to contend with, so prudence and forethought are highly advisable. Do bear in mind that this mark will eventually phase out, giving way to healthier financial conditions.

▬▬▬	*Line of Affection*
▬▬▬	*Line of Fate*
▬▬▬	*Line of Head*
▬▬▬	*Line of Heart*
▬▬▬	*Line of Life*
	Line of the Sun

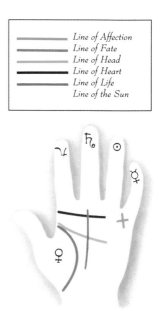

Above. Crosses are often bad news. The one shown here – under the Finger of Mercury ☿ – is particularly negative, as it can show a tendency to be deceptive. Other factors shown here reinforce the cross on Mercury. The Finger of Mercury is not straight, but bends inwards. Generally the straighter this finger, the more straightforward the thinking. The Fingers of Jupiter ♃ and the Sun ☉ are equally long, showing a reckless disposition.

THE ENTREPRENEUR

Below. An entrepreneur's hand. The long Finger of the Sun ☉ shows that the owner enjoys taking chances. The high Mounts of the Sun ☉ and Mercury ☿ show a love of art and communications.

Some people have a talent for making money. They may know when something is of value or when a situation can be used advantageously. Such people are often known as entrepreneurs.

How this aptitude works in people's lives can vary greatly. Enterpreneurs range from the self-made millionaire to the person running a small business. 'Middle men' and agents of all sorts can be included in this category. Such people have the gift of being able to find a means of working in independent, self-employed ways. Sometimes their source of income can be precarious, but such people often enjoy taking chances and can even thrive on the excitement of the challenge and uncertainty. There will usually be an element of the gambler in the entrepreneur in that he or she will take chances and hope to succeed.

The entrepreneur is always an optimist with an enthusiastic disposition. This trait is reflected in the hands, which are likely to be springy and pink. The illustration (see above) shows the hand of someone who thrives on taking risks. Small and fleshy, it also reveals sensuality. The Line of Fate begins on the Mount of the Moon ☽, indicating work involving the public, which could include travelling. It forks, sending one branch to Saturn ♄ and one to Jupiter ♃. This reveals powerful ambitions that are likely to be fulfilled.

The Finger of the Sun ☉ is particularly relevant here. If it is very long – longer than the Finger of Jupiter ♃ and nearly as long as the Finger of Saturn ♄ – it can reveal a nature that can be fired with an urge to take big chances. This stems from a positive outlook. If, however, the long Finger of the Sun is found on a hand with a flat Mount of Saturn, a sense of seriousness and responsibility can be lacking. This will be compounded by a changeable Line of Fate.

The Line of the Sun is also linked, among other things, to a positive outlook. Like the Line of Fate, it may not be uniform on an entrepreneur's hand, but meander up the palm in fits and starts. There may be little crossbars on it, which will show where there have been, or will be, financial stumbling blocks to deal with. Such a person may realize some short-term success, but will lack continuity and may even find a secure means of making a living boring because it is predictable. If there is a space between the start of the Lines of Head and Life, and the fingers are flexible with spaces between them at their roots, the personality will be spontaneous. When all these factors are present, especially the long Finger of the Sun ☉, an urge to take chances will be

Above. This spatulate hand reveals a lively, individualistic character. The high Mount of Jupiter ♃ reflects a knack for organizing others.

marked. If the thumb is flexible too, then there can be great generosity.

The Finger and Mount of Mercury ☿ are connected with ideas, communication and, in some instances, commerce and business. The lowest phalange of the entrepreneur's Finger of Mercury will often be longer than the other two because it is associated particularly with business sense. If the Finger of Mercury has a conic or pointed tip, there will be a love of art. When both these features are present, business ability and idealism may combine effectively. A person running an art gallery, for example, often has such fingers. If the Finger of Mercury has a spatulate tip as well as a long lower phalange, then there will be very original ideas that can be financially rewarding. Communications will be energetic.

To be able to see creative potential in others, one would expect to find a Line of Head that slopes towards the Mount of the Moon ☽. If the creative ability will be utilized in practical ways, the slope will not be very steep (see bottom, page 32). The line is also strong and balanced with good powers of self-expression indicated by the fine fork at its end. The developed Mount of Mercury ☿ shows a youthful attitude and a lively mind that can generate lots of ideas. The Line of the Sun fans out on its mount ☉ in several directions. The entrepreneur with this line would be involved in several creative or money-making projects. Between the Lines of Head and Heart, another Line of Fate is to be found, which terminates under the Line of Heart. This can indicate a business venture that was frustrating and fell short of expectations. The heart was, literally, not in it.

Strong, clear Lines of the Sun and Fate with the former emanating from the Mount of the Moon ☽ (see below left) tell of success in dealing with the public in lucrative ways.

A Line of Fate that takes an uncertain course to the Line of Head (see below right) shows poor judgement. In later life, a tendency to financial dissipation will be rendered less acute. This is shown in the Lines of the Sun, which are totally fragmented, but become more defined later. Several Lines of Sun will always create a tendency to wheel and deal uncertainly.

Above. When a little bump stands out on the pad of the thumb, it can contribute to a special tactile sense that can 'feel' the inherent value in an object. People with little, rounded, raised bumps on all their finger pads have tactile abilities in an overall way, but the one on the thumb creates a more specific sense of touch that can be an asset to those interested in objects of art.

Far left. The Fingers of the Sun ☉ and Saturn ♄ are held apart on this hand. This shows that the owner may bend the rules a little in order to exercise a free-spirited approach to life.

Left. A very changeable Line of Fate emanates from the Mount of the Moon ☽ indicating a certain amount of indecision, fluctuating ambitions and perhaps many short journeys. This person could thrive on uncertainty. The Line of Fate breaks below the Line of Head, and resumes with a fork, indicating either a partnership or a career influence. This will probably be an unsuccessful, phase however, because the crossbar shows a major obstacle.

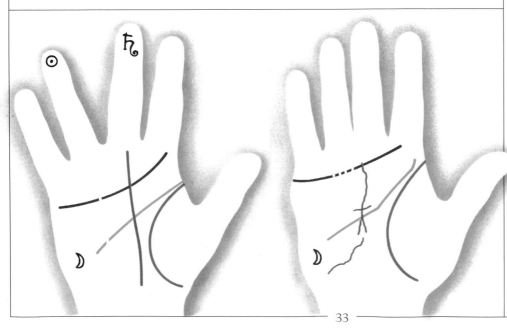

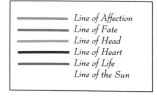

	Line of Affection
	Line of Fate
	Line of Head
	Line of Heart
	Line of Life
	Line of the Sun

DIRECTION AND DEVELOPMENT

Very few people have a totally 'clear run' in their career, or indeed life itself. We all come up against challenges and hurdles. Although these may seem difficult at the time, they are necessary, for as we face them we grow and develop. We are often only truly aware of our inner resources in times of crisis and challenge.

Many people get stuck into a career early in life and do not have the opportunity to taste freedom, to explore the rest of the world through travel, which broadens the horizons of the mind and understanding. Lines of Travel are situated at the lower part of the Mount of the Moon ☽, often an extension of the Line of Life. They are further described in The Outdoor Type (see pages 62-63). A person with many Lines of Travel (see below left) will always have a need to see some of the world, especially if the lines are found mostly

on the left hand. A defined Line of Fate means that there may also be a strong urge to realize a particular career. In early adulthood, there could be a conflict between wanting to 'get on' and needing the freedom to take off and explore other places and possibilities.

Our lives are composed of seven-year cycles (see The Time Factor, pages 38-39). We do not come into our own, in terms of growing up and really defining our personalities and direction, until approximately twenty-eight to thirty years of age. Many people who launch themselves into a career very early on, or marry early, will go through a change of direction at around this age; career or relationships can be redefined in accord with a new adult perspective about life. Think of the people you know whose lives have changed radically at around this age.

Below. This left hand shows the young and restless spirit, needing to see the world.

Below. The right hand shows that the owner is becoming settled and more purposeful.

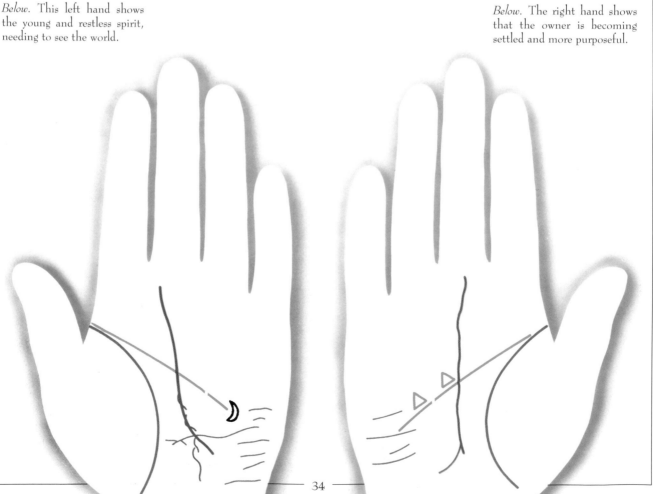

If you are young and want to see some of the world before you finally settle to something, then try to find ways of doing so. Our society puts great emphasis on material security and achievement. This is all very well, but it is also important to experience life and expand one's ideas, especially if you have a fundamental need to travel. If this urge is thwarted and denied, a restless spirit will not be happy in a confined and predictable occupation. There will always be a feeling of dissatisfaction. So if this could be you, do what you need to do now as life is short.

Not everybody has an urge to travel. Some people with a very imaginative (sloping) Line of Head seem to be able to travel on an internal level: they can imagine other places easily so the need to be on the move physically is not urgently felt and they are content to stay at home. Sometimes people who travel as part of their job, such as airline pilots, may not have the urge to travel marked on the palm because it has become an integral part of their daily routine.

The illustrations (see page 34) show the left and right hands of someone who travels a lot when young, but is destined to settle down later on in life. As you can see, the two palms are very different. The left hand, which reveals basic tendencies and the past, shows the need to travel. The right hand, which reveals the future, shows a much more settled life, with a good Line of Fate indicating purposeful direction. There are Lines of Travel on the left hand and the Line of Fate is wavy and spasmodic. This shows that there would have been many short-lived jobs in a variety of places, with the main urge being to travel.

The Line of Fate on the right hand, however, does not meander up the palm. Like the Line of the Sun, it has become well-defined. Purposeful direction will begin to emerge around the late twenties, and as the Line of the Sun corresponds with the Line of Fate in terms of time, the future looks bright and rewarding. Note, too, that the Line of Head has triangles on it, which signify pleasing influences. As the Line of Head is linked to mental ability and capacity, triangles here can reveal something welcome and enjoyable that is being learned.

Although the left hand reveals that the owner of these hands will need to taste some experience of the world early in life, he or she will grow towards a defined sense of purpose later on. The experience of travel will serve to strengthen the personality and to broaden the mind. There is a very pertinent old Arabic saying, 'Experience is the finest ornament'.

A person's family is often a major source of difficulty that may not be easy to overcome. If the problem is severe, it can thwart the ability of a young person to define a personal sense of direction and ambition in life (see Family and Career, pages 36-37).

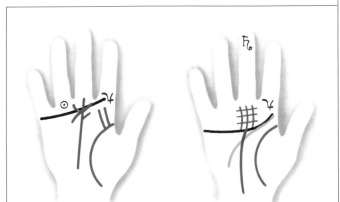

Above. Obstacles are indicated here by a line crossing over the end of the Line of Fate. Two other lines branch from the Line of Fate, one veering towards the Mount of the Sun ☉ and the other directed towards the Mount of Jupiter ♃. These branches are positive signs. Two Lines of Ambition rise from the Line of Life to the Mount of Jupiter. In this case, ambitions can be strong, but some diversity of interest will create the contradictory line crossing the Line of Fate. There may be 'too many irons in the fire' of the career but, as the Line of Fate is so well-defined, things will definitely improve eventually.

Above. A grille anywhere on the palm indicates problems of a temporary nature. Here, it is found at the end of the Line of Fate, which tells of a period of delays and thwarted aims connected with work or the main line of interest. Patience and optimism will be necessary for a while but the influence is not permanent. In some cases this grille formation on the Mount of Saturn ♄ links with depressive tendencies (see pages 110-111). For an otherwise positive individual, however, a worrying time will not become a state of permanent negativity. Note also how the Line of Head begins close to the Mount of Jupiter ♃, which indicates very ambitious ideas.

Line of Affection	Line of Heart
Line of Fate	Line of Life
Line of Head	Line of the Sun

Family and career

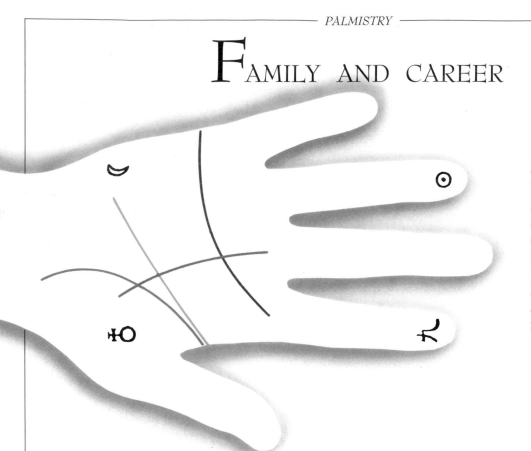

Our career can be influenced enormously, positively or otherwise, by our family. For some people, independence from the family can be difficult for various reasons. The Line of Fate is an important factor here.

An independent Line of Fate stands away from the Line of Life and the Mount of the Moon ☽. The nearer the wrist and middle of the palm it begins, the earlier a self-reliant attitude to life would have been realized. If the Line of Fate begins inside (not on) the Line of Life, on the Mount of Venus ♀, there will be dependence on the family (see above). Such a tendency will be marked, showing a person with rather a weak disposition who will happily lean on the family, if any of the following features are also present: a soft, malleable hand; a thumb with a small, weak-looking upper section that does not feel very resistant when you try to bend it back gently; an underdeveloped Mount of Jupiter ♃; and a Finger of Jupiter that is noticeably shorter than that of the Sun ☉.

It is important that you remember to examine both hands. If you were to find the above features on the left hand, but the right showed a more independent Line of Fate, then you could assume that the subject would eventually be able to stand on his or her own two feet in life. As the left hand corresponds with basic tendencies, however, the need to lean on others to some extent is never likely to disappear completely.

Sometimes the Lines of Fate and Life begin separately but, later on, the Line of Fate veers towards and mingles with the Line of Life, subsequently resuming its separate course up the hand (see above right). This indicates that, for some reason, there will be family influences that interfere with life, work or both. Family issues will come to the fore, demanding time and attention. One's career will have to be temporarily shelved, or at least take second place, while the Line of Fate is caught up with the Line of Life. Examine the Mount of Venus ♀. If you find small crosses close to the area where the two lines join, there

Line of Affection		Line of Heart
Line of Fate		Line of Life
Line of Head		Line of the Sun

may be some sort of family crisis, such as an illness. A move back into the family home may be necessary.

A Line of Fate emanating from the edge of the Mount of the Moon ☽ is also significant to family and career (see bottom, near right). As this mount is associated with emotions and the past, a line such as this can mean that there will be strong family attachments and memories of childhood. If the Mount of Moon is very developed and the hand is soft, flaccid and damp, there will be overt sentiment and sometimes nostalgia for the past. This may not be very realistic as the owner may fantasize about what has been, preferring to dream of the past than live in the present. Such an attitude could dilute independence. Sometimes this can mean there are manipulative influences from family members, who may exert an emotional hold on a child into adulthood, not allowing it to feel free.

Marriage – or a close relationship – and children can bring a sense of direction. For some people, these commitments come relatively late in life. Look for a weak Line of Fate that becomes clearer half-way or even higher up the palm, or a Line of Fate that manifests on the right but not on the left hand. When the new feeling of responsibility is due to children or a dependent partner, this is shown by a Line of Influence rising to join the newly emerging Line of Fate.

Below. Family matters are shown here, tugging at the Line of Fate, temporarily interfering with the career or other aspects of life.

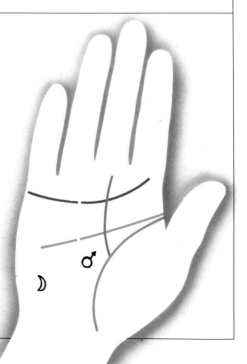

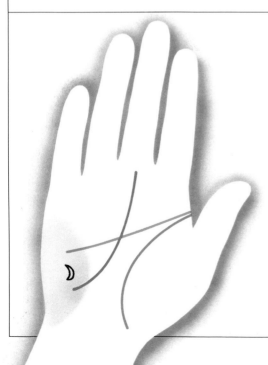

Left. Here the Line of Fate begins within a very developed Mount of the Moon ☽. This shows that emotional and family factors can inhibit an independent stance in life.

Right. The Line of Fate begins on (not within) the Line of Life. There is unlikely to be much help from the family and there may be a difficult start in life. The Line of Fate rises boldly up the hand, however, bringing independence and success. The Line of the Sun touches neither the Line of Life nor the Mount of the Moon ☽. It emanates from the Plain of Mars ♂ and shows positive determination.

THE TIME FACTOR

'When would be a good time to make my next career move?' People often ask me this when they come for a reading. Work dominates most of our lives, so people are naturally keen to find out when career changes are likely to come about.

You can find out when events in your life will occur by consulting the lines on the palm. A knowledge of time as shown on the hands is very important for every palmist. When you are carrying out a reading, it is all very well predicting an important life event, but this will be frustrating for the subject if you cannot say roughly when it is likely to happen. Here I will show you how to read the lines in terms of time; and then on pages 40–41 I will show how certain marks, when found on a line, can predict the timing of an event.

Before you begin to study time as shown on the hands, you must be familiar with the meanings of each of the major lines. Practise reading the character and predispositions as revealed on the hand before going on to time events, or you could get into a muddle, especially if you have never tried to study palmistry before.

The next step is to learn at which end each line starts. This is because each line literally represents a lifespan, with the beginning of the line corresponding with the early years of life. The Line of Life is read downwards towards the wrist. The Lines of the Sun and Fate are read upwards. The Line of Head is read from the end nearest the thumb. The Line of Heart begins at the end nearest the Finger of Mercury ☿.

You will see from the illustrations that each line is marked at seven-year intervals. This is because physically, mentally and emotionally we change every seven years. Most lines you will come across will not be the same length as the ones shown here. Long lines can still be divided up into equal seven-year intervals, making slight adjustments to allow for the length of each line. Shorter lines are more difficult. You might, for example, see a Line of Fate that begins half-way up the palm. In order to gauge timing in this case, draw a line, either with a pen or in your imagination, from the usual starting place of the Line of Fate at the bot-

tom of the hand up to where it actually starts. Then fill in the seven-year intervals as usual along the whole line. This will reveal the age at which the line comes into effect.

Timing events correctly takes practice. It is a good idea to start by asking your subject to talk about an important event he or she has experienced, and then see if you can find it on the relevant line on the palm. You could try this using your own palm, but bear in mind that it can be difficult to be totally objective about oneself.

Always begin a reading by finding out the age of your subject. This will enable you to distinguish between past, present and future events. Sometimes people will not tell the truth about their age, usually pretending to be younger. This can affect

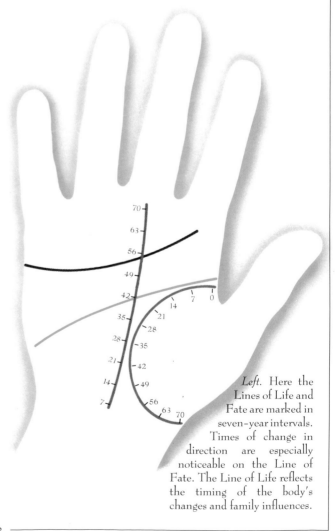

Left. Here the Lines of Life and Fate are marked in seven-year intervals. Times of change in direction are especially noticeable on the Line of Fate. The Line of Life reflects the timing of the body's changes and family influences.

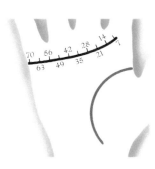

Above. The Line of Heart reveals a person's emotional and sex life. This is the line that shows years when one is happy or sad. Certain marks on this line reflect turbulent periods within close relationships, as well as times of great joy. Above all, this is the line that shows times of love. As people tend to be more interested in their love life than anything else, you are likely to consult this line a lot when reading the hands in terms of time.

Below. The Line of the Sun is generally positive. It is linked to sensitivity to the environment, creativity, success and, frequently, to financial matters. You can time positive, satisfying events and financial benefits from this line.

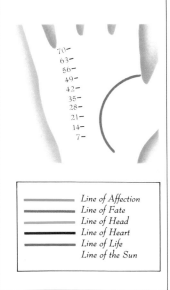

————	Line of Affection
————	Line of Fate
————	Line of Head
————	Line of Heart
————	Line of Life
————	Line of the Sun

the accuracy of your predictions, but that is their problem, not yours.

Remember that the left and right hands are never exactly the same. The left hand shows basic tendencies and past events, whilst the right shows how these tendencies change and develop and what is still to come. Bear in mind, too, that the lines on the diagrams shown here may not always correspond with the lines on the hands, so make allowances for differences. Some hands will have one or even two absent lines.

The Line of Fate is particularly helpful in gauging the timing of life's events. Whatever happens in life often shows more clearly on this line than on any other, because it reveals our route, goal and destiny. It is a major indicator of drive and energies and mirrors our lives more succinctly than the other lines. It therefore demands special attention when addressing the timing of major events. As it is concerned with career matters, it will also show changes in jobs, set-backs and triumphs. There are often other lines to be found interacting with the Line of Fate. These reveal people or events that are instrumental in our direction and purpose. Not everyone has a Line of Fate. Other people have a line that is not easily decipherable. When this is the case, pay attention to the other lines, particularly the Line of Life.

Some hands do not seem to have a Line of Heart, or it may look as though the Line of Head is missing. Where there are usually two lines, there is only one. This is the Simian Line (see pages 90-91), a combination of the Lines of Head and Heart. Read it as you would the Line of Heart.

A seemingly short Line of Life can be viewed with fear and alarm, but it is rarely possible to predict the demise of a person from this line. Many people dread having their hands read, mistakenly thinking that a cursory glance will reveal the exact moment of death, and that it could be imminent. This is definitely not so. The Line of Life is about life, vitality, travel and, to some degree, love and affection. It also reflects the constitution and can show potential illness, but a short line does not, by itself, show a short lifespan.

On some palms, the Line of Life 'moves over' towards the centre of the hand. To the untrained eye, this can look like another line altogether. This can happen when a person literally moves away to go and live in another country for example.

Some people look as if they have two Lines of Life. The second line, closest to the thumb side, gives added strength and resistance. This is a fortunate line: it takes the strain of problems and illness and allows a person to bounce back into life after any health or other difficulties. When a double line is found, regard the outer one as the Line of Life.

Hands with a lot of lines all over them can present a great puzzle to the novice palmist. Identifying each line can be difficult, let alone trying to time important events. A complex hand is likely to belong to a complicated personality. If you find yourself at a loss as to where to begin, do not attempt to read the lines, or to time any events until you are more experienced, or you will make mistakes and feel discouraged. Start by concentrating on hands with fewer, clearer lines. Remember that women tend to have more complex, lined hands than men. It can be a good idea to use a very fine-tipped pen to map out the seven year intervals on the lines. Do this on one line at a time until you are more practised.

TIMING MAJOR EVENTS

Getting to grips with timing major events by examining the palm can be tricky. In The Time Factor (see pages 38-39) I described the basic principles. Here I will carry out two 'case history' sample readings, to show you exactly how much information there is to be found out about time from the palms.

Joe's hand

This is Joe's left hand (see below), so it will show his basic tendencies and what has happened in the past. When looking at the hand in terms of time, always start by identifying the main points of the personality. This will help you put major events in their true context.

Next, examine the Line of Fate, the most significant line in terms of reflecting major events. It starts clearly and decisively, but changes a lot as it rises up the palm. What happened?

In his early twenties, Joe got married to a girl he had known since childhood. Towards the beginning of the Line of Fate, there is a Line of Influence from the left, which leans towards the Line of Fate and then crosses its path. This shows that the marriage was not happy. Joe's partner was not able to help him in supportive ways. As this Line of Influence cuts rather than blends with the Line of Fate, the marriage would have been fraught with problems right from the start. But Joe loved his wife. His idealism, capacity for love and his sympathetic thinking always enabled him to forgive her, even when she was difficult and tempestuous. But things got worse and worse.

Look at the lower Line of Affection, situated below the Finger of Mercury ☿ and closest to the Line of Heart. This line represents Joe's marriage. You can see that the line splits, revealing that there was an actual split in the relationship. Note that the split occurs fairly early on in the line, corresponding with the twenty-seventh year, which was Joe's age when his wife walked out on him. Note how the Line of Fate forks. This is often an indication of separation and major change in life's circumstances. Joe and his difficult and often hostile partner got back together again briefly. Joe could not stop loving her. When she returned, he loved her more than ever, but one day she simply disappeared.

See how the lower Line of Affection, after splitting, sends a line down to touch the Line of Head. This indicates the terrific shock Joe had when the one he loved went away, made worse by not knowing where she was or if anything had happened to her. Poor Joe was so distraught that every aspect of his life culminated in crisis. The island on the Line of Life shows that the trauma affected his health. On the split Line of Fate, the island indicates that there was a corresponding critical period in his career. For a while Joe felt as if he was losing his grip on life, for his missing wife had meant so much to him. The Line of Mars helped Joe to recover from this dreadful time. As you can see, his Line of Fate starts up again after the split.

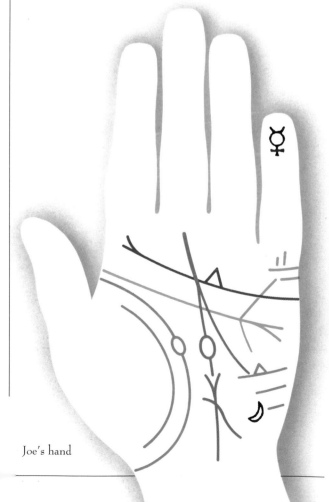

Joe's hand

A liking for travel is shown by the Lines of Travel on the Mount of the Moon ☽. When Joe was thirty, he went to Thailand and met a beautiful girl. She returned with him to be married. The happiness he found in meeting her is shown in the triangle on the Line of Travel and in the second, clear Line of Affection. The Line of Influence rising from the Line of Travel blends in with the Line of Fate. A triangle on the Line of Heart showing happiness is also found at around this period in Joe's life.

When Joe was thirty-five, he and his wife opened a Thai restaurant. It was a success. Note how the Line of Sun, which denotes good fortune, starts at the point on the palm representing Joe's age at this time. Joe and his wife had a good life. They had two children: a boy and a girl.

Margaret's hand

This is the hand of a sensitive woman (see right). Note the long, conic fingers. She is strong-willed, indicated by the firm thumb. The space between the Lines of Head and Life reveals confidence, impulsiveness, a broad-minded attitude and a sense of humour. The Line of Head forks at the end, a feature that enhances mental balance and self-expression. The upper line of the fork branches towards the Mount of Mercury ☿, revealing an interest in making money.

Margaret has a Girdle of Venus. Like a secondary Line of Heart, it begins between the Fingers of Saturn ♄ and Jupiter ♃, and ends between the Fingers of the Sun ☉ and Mercury ☿. This tells of a volatile, creative response to life.

There are four Lines of Children on Margaret's palm, three girls and a boy. The eldest child, the boy, is represented by the longest Line of Children, close to the outer edge of the palm. Note that there is a triangle on the Family Ring at the base of the thumb. This tells of much pleasure in family life. As the Family Ring is neat and uniform, there is a strong sense of responsibility towards the family.

Now let us look at a time of potentially major crisis in her life. The cross on her Line of Life corresponds with the thirty-seventh year of life. It is interesting that the cross on the Line of Fate occurs at the same time. Around the age of thirty-

seven, Margaret could be involved in an accident. Note that the Line of Head is also affected by the cross on the Line of Fate, showing that the accident may not only affect the physical body (as shown in the Line of Life) but also, temporarily, her mind. Squares cover the crosses, serving to protect Margaret from serious injury, and to ensure a speedy recovery. The cross on the Line of Fate indicates a break in career while a full recovery is made. Crosses covered by a square on the Line of Life often mean an accident as opposed to a health problem.

Margaret is a spontaneous person. She will rush at things, often without thinking of the consequences of her actions. This makes her a little accident-prone. But in this case, she may have unconsciously created an accident in order to have some rest and attention.

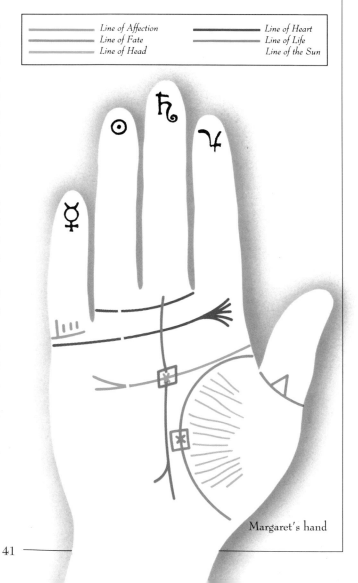

Line of Affection	Line of Heart
Line of Fate	Line of Life
Line of Head	Line of the Sun

Margaret's hand

CAREER CHANGES AND BREAKS

Most people experience a break or change in career at some point in life. Such phases can be exciting, opening doors to new opportunity; or they can be traumatic, the result of forces beyond our control. Palmistry can show you when changes are likely to happen, how you can respond to them and what new direction may come. The Line of Fate is particularly relevant here, as it is to all career matters.

We live in a worrying period as far as career matters are concerned. Everything is changing rapidly and the possibility of redundancy hangs like a threatening black cloud over the lives of many people. To lose one's source of income can be catastrophic, but life will still go on. It is important to bear in mind that when we have such big upheavals in our lives, we usually manage to adjust and reorientate ourselves successfully. Unexpected changes, especially in relation to work, do not have to be experienced negatively. Many of us are in unsuitable careers that make us feel cribbed and frustrated, so an enforced change can feel like being let out of prison.

Look at the illustration (top right). The break in this Line of Fate shows a change in career happening around the thirty-third year (see pages 38-41 for an explanation of the hands and time). Where the Line of Fate breaks, there are two lines on either side, known as 'sister' lines. These are very helpful here, serving as sort of scaffolding poles that keep everything shored up whilst changes are in progress. They can manifest as supportive people or other influences. At the end of the Line of Head there is a blurred patch, indicating mental fatigue likely to be caused by anxiety. Fine bars crossing the Line of Head can correspond with a time of deep anxiety. Examine the line itself: if it is very finely etched onto the palm and the lines crossing it are heavier than the line itself, the degree of anxiety will be marked. Do bear in mind that these little lines are of a temporary nature. Happily, the Line of Fate eventually starts up again, life goes on and a full recovery from challenging, and probably enforced, changes will be realized. We all tend to fear

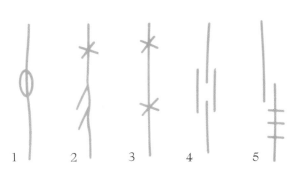

Above. 1. Islands indicate bothersome influences or people. 2. Crosses on the Line of Life show illness; drooping lines reveal lassitude. 3. Crosses on the Mount of Saturn ♄ at the end of the Line of Fate mean temporary problems. 4. 'Sister' lines help to lend support in times of change. 5. Crossbars show obstacles, often corresponding with delays.

Below. There is a good, clear Line of Fate on this hand, but notice the island upon it. This mark usually corresponds with a short-lived but irritating situation. There may, for example, be problems with colleagues, or the job itself may feel tedious. At the end of the Line of Fate there is a grille of criss-cross lines. Again, this indicates a temporary, though uncomfortable, influence that will negate drive and progress. When this is found on the right hand, it is inadvisable to make any changes as they will not work out well. As the marks fade, normal progress will be resumed.

Above. This Line of Life has crosses and drooping lines upon it. In this context, the crosses show illness, and the drooping lines, lassitude. We are all ill from time to time and forced to take time off work. The Line of Fate comes to a temporary halt whilst the illness runs its course, but starts up again with renewed vigour. If such crosses are found on the right hand and energies are low, it would be a good idea to have a medical check-up. Any potential illness may not be severe, so do not panic. The crosses can remind you to take good care of yourself.

change, even when it is the thing we need most. Progress can only come about through change. When you look back at times in your life when you were on the brink of some new and uncertain phase, you may realize that your fears were unfounded.

Now look at the illustration (bottom right). This Line of Fate, which has crossbars upon it, stops beneath the Line of Head but a new line overlaps and supersedes it. These markings show that a change will occur over a period of time and usually out of choice. Progress has been limited by an earlier inability to realize the unsuitability of a career. There could have been a reluctance to change due to a stubborn stance, or even a lack of confidence, creating a 'better-the-devil-you-know' attitude. As the Lines of Fate begin to overlap, the urge to do something will come into effect and the transition will be well met. As the second Line of Fate begins at a slight distance from the former one, a new sort of career and fresh aims are likely. A Line of the Sun begins around the same place as the second Line of Fate, telling of satisfaction and success in a new direction.

Computer technology is now beginning to release people from soul-destroying and tedious occupations. We are immersed in times of irrevocable transitions that will touch all our lives, but most of us are not yet sufficiently well-prepared for our new world. It is therefore a good idea to be prepared to consider training options and to develop other skills and interests.

Many of us spend much of our lives working and find it difficult to make the most of our free time. This kind of life-style can negatively affect the mind, body and spirit. Using leisure time effectively is a sure way to enhance quality of life.

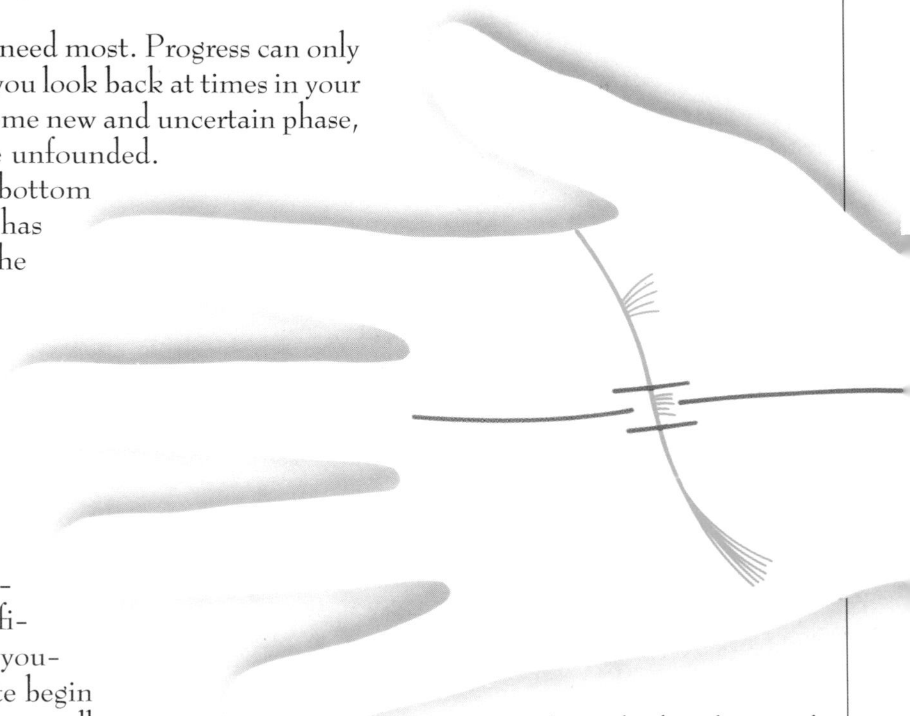

Below. Limitation has been self-inflicted in this case, but a change in attitude allows a new direction to be reached for. A fresh sense of future possibilities and of confidence will be forthcoming.

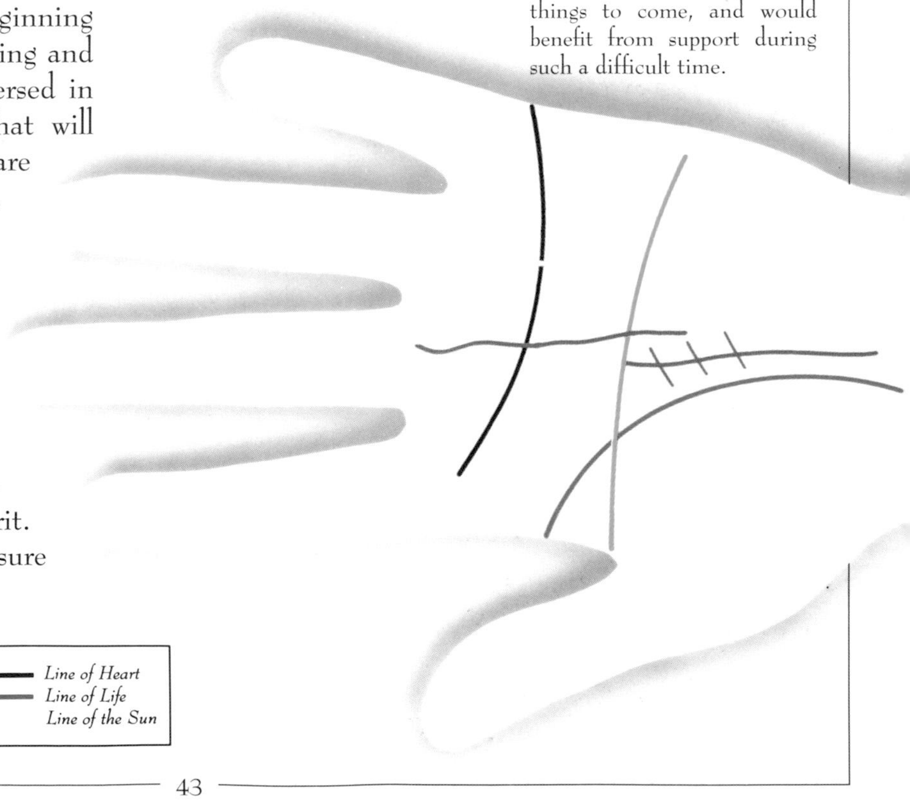

Above. A break in the Line of Fate will always mean a change in career or other main line of interest. It does not have to be a radical change. Changes fraught with anxiety are shown by drooping hair lines and a blurred look to the end of the Line of Head. The owner may need to cultivate faith in better things to come, and would benefit from support during such a difficult time.

Line of Affection		Line of Heart
Line of Fate		Line of Life
Line of Head		Line of the Sun

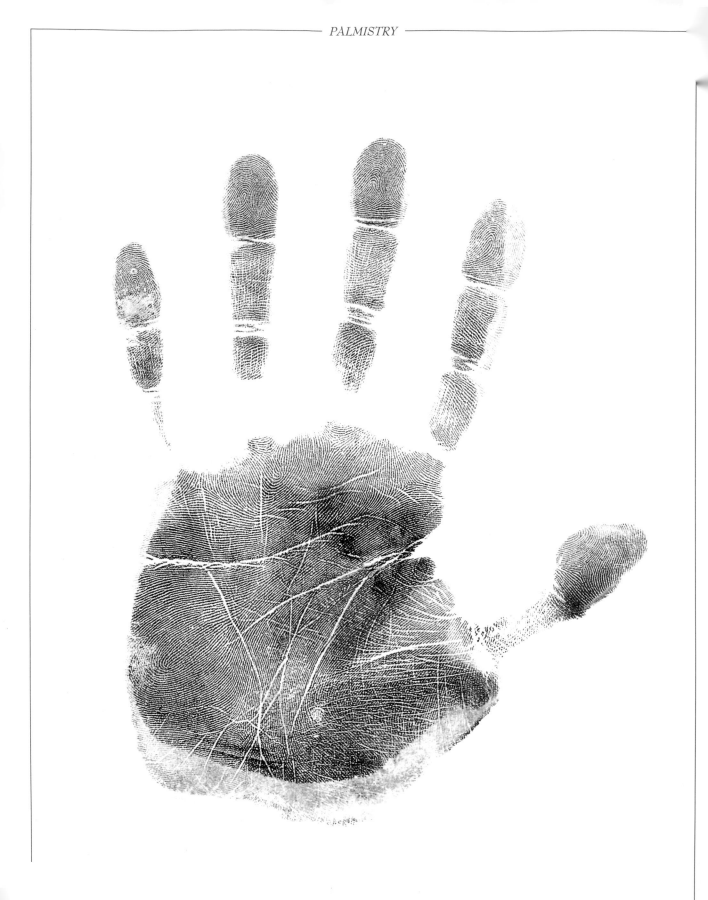

Michael's hand (life-size)

SAMPLE READING
MICHAEL'S HAND

This is the left palm of a thirty-five-year-old man. As he is left-handed, this palm should be treated as the 'right' hand in that it reveals present and future conditions. Michael is a self-employed antique dealer, and has been involved in other business ventures.

Firstly, note the length of the fingers in relation to one another. The Fingers of the Sun and Jupiter are equal in length and both are nearly as long as the Finger of Saturn. This shows that Michael enjoys taking chances.

Michael's Lines of Life and Head are separate, indicating spontaneity. His Line of Head dips gently towards the Mount of the Moon, suggesting that his thinking is imaginative. You can see that the Mount of the Moon is high and well-formed, which enhances creative feelings and ideas. On a less positive note, however, it can also make him a little moody sometimes.

Next, let us examine his Line of Fate. Look carefully at its starting point: it rises from just inside the Line of Life, almost imperceptibly brushing the Mount of Venus. This indicates that there are two factors that govern his career: the Line of Fate rising from the Line of Life shows that he is a self-starter. This feature is often found on the palms of self-employed people. As the Line of Fate also touches the Mount of Venus, albeit slightly, it means that his family has been, and will continue to be, very linked to his career, though he is not dependent on them. Note that the top phalange of the Finger of Mercury is longer than those of the other fingers, revealing a great capacity for communication.

One of the most prominent features on this palm is the Line of Intuition. It is quite rare to find the line as well-formed as it is here. It helps Michael to assess situations and other people intuitively. He often acts on hunches that bring benefits to his business life. Although he is not academic, he understands ideas and information very quickly, and enjoys the sort of situations that challenge his mind.

Michael's Line of the Sun is interesting as well. It is very clear as it passes the Line of Heart, but notice the fainter and less-defined portion below, rising in barely discernible fits and starts. This reveals that there have been, and will continue to be for some time, shaky business interactions as well as times of prosperity and success. As this line is well-defined from the Line of Heart onwards, Michael will realize a deeper sense of satisfaction in his life, probably with more settled financial conditions, as he gets older.

There are two defined branches from the Line of Fate. These often indicate two strings to the bow of the career or main line of interest. On Michael's hand, they change as they reach up to the Line of Head. In terms of time, this corresponds approximately with the thirty-fifth year. One branch terminates under the Line of Head and the other just crosses it. At the same juncture, a little line rises from the Line of Head, crossing the Line of Fate and heading towards the Mount of the Sun. The Line of Fate above it then changes course slightly, emanating from a tiny triangle. This indicates that an idea will be forthcoming that will bring new direction to the career, and that the ability to focus on ambitions will be clearer. The Line of Fate will pass over the Line of Heart, meaning that what he does will not feel frustrating or thwarting.

To sum up, Michael's hand shows that he has made and spent a lot of money. He is very interested in making it, but is not motivated through greed or acquisitiveness alone. For him, challenges are important. He enjoys applying his quick and intuitive thinking to situations. He is an opportunist, and will be able to assess a situation rapidly that may be lucrative. At the time of writing, he is feeling a little uncertain about long-term direction in his life. He knows intuitively that there will be changes, that he is poised on the brink of a new way of working, but has not yet defined what it may be. All this is indicated by the Line of Fate.

COMMON QUESTIONS

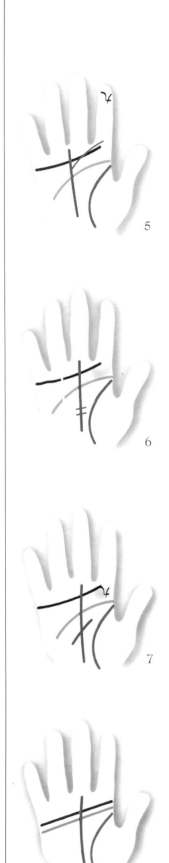

1. I would like to invest money. Is it a good time for me to do this?
   Now is not a good time as there is a cross on your Mount of the Sun ⊙. As this is usually a temporary mark, wait until it disappears.

2. I am fed up with my job and want to be an artist. Is this a feasible course of action?
   Your double Line of Fate suggests that you may pursue two careers. Your good Line of the Sun shows that you have talent.

3. Will my family help my career financially?
   Probably. Your Line of the Sun emanates from the Mount of Venus ♀ indicating likely family help. Try to not be too dependent on them.

4. I fear I may lose my job. Will I be able to cope and to find another one?
   Do not worry. Although the small cross shows trepidation, your Line of Fate reveals positive change. A new line overlaps the break, reflecting a smooth transition to a new phase in your life.

5. I have been offered a managerial post. Will I be confident enough to be in charge?
   Your Line of Fate branches to Jupiter ♃, indicating authority and ambition. Take the promotion.

6. My work is presently full of obstacles. Should I follow my wish to give it up?
   Battle on! The crossbars on your Line of Fate and the island on your Line of the Sun show only temporary frustrations. Things will improve soon.

7. I want to leave my job because I hate my boss. Is this a good idea?
   You have a troublesome, interfering crossbar on your Line of Fate. Your large Mount of Jupiter ♃ means you have an innate need to assert yourself. Try to be patient, or look for another job.

8. Sometimes I feel trapped by work and responsibility. Why is this?
   Your narrow quadrangle shows you can take everything, not just work, too seriously.

9. I am considering taking a transfer to an office in a new area. Is this a good idea?
   A branch from the Line of Fate to Mercury ☿, which often links with movement, and a happy triangle suggests that it is indeed a good idea.

9

10

11

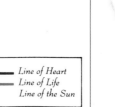

12

10. I am thirty years old but my life lacks a defined direction. Will this change?
Yes. Your Lines of Fate and the Sun strengthen. You will feel well-motivated and happy soon.

11. I am thinking of going on a course to improve my qualifications. It will cost me quite a lot of money. Will I enjoy it?
Your long Line of Head and a triangle on Mercury ☿ suggest that you will enjoy and succeed in learning new skills. The course will be well worth the money.

12. Recently I had an inspired idea for making money. In my excitement, I told a friend about it. Was I unwise to do so?
Probably. A line from the Mount of Mars ♂ crossing your Line of the Sun shows potential jealousy and interference. Watch out!

13. I am planning an exciting new business venture. Unfortunately, things keep going wrong. What is the reason for this?
There is a grille on your Mount of Mercury ☿, which shows general short-term difficulty. Although it might not be possible, shelving any plans until the grille disappears would be wise.

14. My wife would like to be involved in my business. I am a bit apprehensive about it. Would this arrangement work for us?
You have a very happy Line of Affection, which represents your marriage. There are no signs of problems in your relationship, so try working together.

15. I gamble. I win and lose. My dream is to be rich eventually. Will it come true?
Your long Fingers of the Sun ☉ and Jupiter ♃ show recklessness. Rather than an indication of good fortune, severe loss is shown in the cross on the Line of the Sun. Be careful. Try to give up if you can.

16. I have yet another great business idea. I know this one could succeed. Should I follow my instincts and start putting my plans into action?
Be realistic. Look at the performance of your previous ideas. There are many lines on the Mount of the Sun ☉, which show you have too many irons in the fire of your career and finances. Research your idea thoroughly before you commit any money to it.

13

14

15

16

	Line of Affection		Line of Heart
	Line of Fate		Line of Life
	Line of Head		Line of the Sun

Chapter Three

TALENT AND POTENTIAL

Everybody has something! Palmistry can help to show where your talents are to be found and how best to utilize them.

Many people, especially when young, have great potential. Unless the spark is recognized, encouraged and nurtured its little light grows dim, although it does not always go out altogether.

We all need education. Gifted children, however, can lose touch with their budding talent if it becomes submerged beneath education systems that do not allow in-dividiual needs to grow and blossom creatively. Perhaps this applies to you.

Do you feel you have lost touch with your gift or talent? There is no time like the present to rekindle the spark, so think of what you know you can do, or what you would like to do, and do it!

In this chapter you will find out about special marks, lines or other features on your palm that correspond with your abilities. People who apply themselves to developing their gifts always tend to feel happier and more satisfied than those who do not, so be good to yourself and light up your true potential.

THE ARTISTIC HAND

There are countless ways in which people find expression through art. Potters, painters and sculptors will have different lines and features on the palm to reflect their choice of medium. All artists, however, have certain similarities on the palm, which will be examined here.

Venus is the planet associated with beauty and love. Most artists have a full Mount of Venus ♀; the more developed this is, the more artistic and also emotional the temperament is likely to be. If, therefore, the mount is very pronounced in relation to the rest of the palm, the creative sensitivity can be fiery and impassioned.

The illustration (right) shows an artistic hand with a full Mount of Venus ♀. The fingers are long and conic, often a feature of painters' hands. The Finger of the Sun ☉ is relatively long. Its square tip shows practicality; the owner will be able to use talent in a constructive way. A high Mount of the Sun can also be seen on this hand, which is fairly uncommon, and amplifies a person's innermost abilities, especially in the artistic sense. When the Mounts of the Sun and Venus are both full, the owner will have a very strong sense of colour and light. The Mount of Jupiter ♃ is usually fairly well developed on the hand of an artist, adding a sense of confidence.

As a rule, artistic people will have a sloping Line of Head. The straighter this line, the more linear and practical will be the thinking. When it slopes towards the Mount of the Moon ☽, it shows a strong imagination.

The illustration (right) shows a hand with knotty joints. These are often found on the hands of artists, showing a tendency to pay attention to detail. The Line of Head slopes gently towards the Mount of the Moon ☽, but self-expression will always take time because the knotty joints dam the creative flow with thought.

A curved line linking the Mounts of Saturn ♄ and the Sun ☉ is called the Girdle of Venus (see above). Not always a complete semi-circle, it enables a person to be creatively attuned to the environment and the people in it. It also gives a boost to vitality. An artist with this line will be

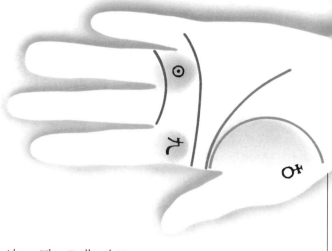

Above. The Girdle of Venus used to be described as an indication of uncontrollable sexual urges. What it really brings, however, is a lusty, electric and often original quality to creative work and other aspects of life.

——————	Line of Affection
——————	Line of Fate
——————	Line of Head
——————	Line of Heart
——————	Line of Life
——————	Line of the Sun

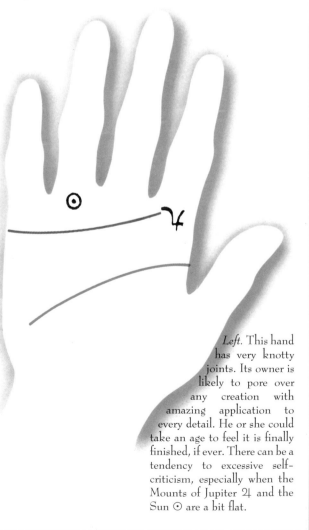

Left. This hand has very knotty joints. Its owner is likely to pore over any creation with amazing application to every detail. He or she could take an age to feel it is finally finished, if ever. There can be a tendency to excessive self-criticism, especially when the Mounts of Jupiter ♃ and the Sun ☉ are a bit flat.

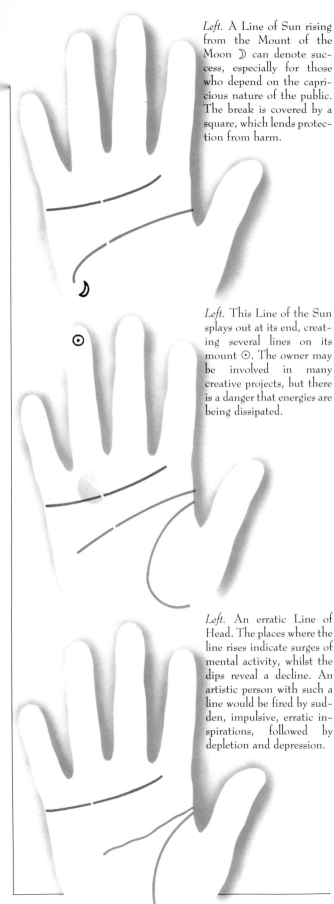

Left. A Line of Sun rising from the Mount of the Moon ☽ can denote success, especially for those who depend on the capricious nature of the public. The break is covered by a square, which lends protection from harm.

Left. This Line of the Sun splays out at its end, creating several lines on its mount ☉. The owner may be involved in many creative projects, but there is a danger that energies are being dissipated.

Left. An erratic Line of Head. The places where the line rises indicate surges of mental activity, whilst the dips reveal a decline. An artistic person with such a line would be fired by sudden, impulsive, erratic inspirations, followed by depletion and depression.

able to infuse creative work with sensitivity, insight and enthusiasm. Many palmists associate this line with volatile sexual responses. Artists may find that it lends excitement to their work.

When there is much space between the Lines of Life and Head, an impulsive disposition is likely. The wider this space, the more spontaneous the actions will be. There are several Lines of the Sun on its mount ☉, showing 'too many irons in the fire' and not enough focus on one idea or project. The sloping Line of Head shows much imagination, so the owner of this hand will constantly be dreaming up new creations and then rushing to do them in an impulsive way. Self-control and discipline may need a lot of cultivation.

Sculptors tend to have strong hands. Like most artists, their Mount of Venus ♀ will be developed; and as the work is more tactile than painting or drawing, the fingers will tend to be spatulate with a broad palm. The illustration (below) shows such a hand. Note the developed Mount of Mars ♂, bringing determined physical effort. The Mount of the Moon ☽ is also developed, showing that the owner is in touch with the imagination.

When a person is undergoing some kind of physical limitation, such as a prison sentence or illness, previously undeveloped creative abilities sometimes come to the fore. Many people have untapped creative talents. If you were good at art as a child, why not see if you can still be in touch with what you had? You may not become another Picasso, but you could gain a great deal of pleasure for yourself and, perhaps, for others.

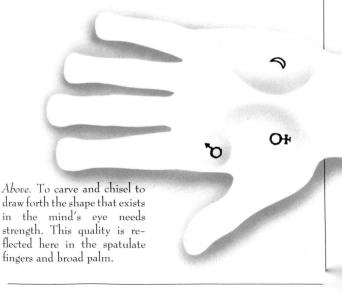

Above. To carve and chisel to draw forth the shape that exists in the mind's eye needs strength. This quality is reflected here in the spatulate fingers and broad palm.

THE PERFORMER

The urge to act, or somehow perform to an audience, can manifest in various ways on the hand. The archetypal actor's hand (see below) will tend to be conic in shape with long, smooth fingers. There will be spaces between the fingers, and the hand as a whole will have a springy feeling to it with a flexible thumb.

Most creative people have some sort of Line of the Sun. The presence of this line does not necessarily mean the person is artistic, but he or she will be sensitive to the environment and in touch with positive inner energies. This line is often found on successful hands.

The performer's Finger of Jupiter ♃ is often long, denoting confidence. The top phalange of the Finger of Mercury ☿ is long in relation to the other finger tops. Mercury is the finger of communication so a long tip shows the ability to talk persuasively. The Mount of Jupiter is often developed on the hands of actors or others who have an urge to place themselves in front of others and perform somehow. The need to 'show off' and have an audience can apply to many professions other than the stage, such as politics and the priesthood. Lawyers and actors generally have very similar hands. This is because both professions depend on their ability to persuade and sway their audience through the powers of oratory and personality.

People with the ability to command and hold the attention of others are likely to have well-developed Mounts of the Moon ☽ and Venus ♀, as well as Jupiter ♃. If there is a good, clear Line of the Sun stemming from the Mount of the Moon, it can add much likeable charm to the personality, even contributing to good looks, or giving an illusion of such, through charisma. Charismatic performers may not always have the ability to act, sing or otherwise entertain with any remarkable gift or talent, but they have attractive and sometimes mesmerizing personalities to which people respond. You can probably think of some famous performers whose success is due to a rather larger-than-life character but whose actual talents are not so incredible.

A sloping Line of Head with branches turning up towards the Finger and Mount of Mercury ☿ at its end reveals a particular talent for communicating ideas creatively. The lower branch towards the edge of the hand can increase the ability to be calculating and to use a convincing performance for one's own ends, on or off the stage. An actor, or aspiring thespian, without a sloping Line of Head may still be able to project the personality well and perform convincingly, but the ability to be immersed in a role and take on another personality, as most great actors do, will not be so forthcoming. Actors also need an excellent memory as they have so many lines to remember. People with a good ability for recollection generally have a well-marked Line of Fate rather than one cut lightly into the palm.

Below. An actor's hand. The fingers are conic, long and smooth and there are well-developed Mounts of Venus ♀, the Moon ☽ and Jupiter ♃, together with a Line of the Sun and a sloping Line of Head. There is a long finger of Jupiter and a long top phalange on the Finger of Mercury ☿.

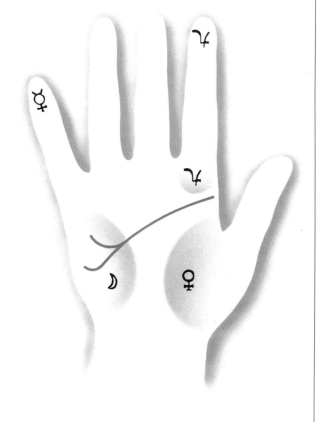

There are many characteristics on a lawyer's hand that correspond to that of an actor (see top right), such as the long Finger and high Mount of Jupiter ♃, denoting confidence and a strong ego. There will also be a high Mount of Mercury ☿. The Finger of Mercury will have a long top phalange in relation to the other fingers and there will usually be a good Line of Fate and Sun. The Line of Head will slope slightly towards the Mount of the Moon ☽. The thumb often stands away from the rest of the hand and has a long, wide top.

The right and left hands of an actor may be quite different. There may be a very sloping Line of Head on the left hand, showing a basically creative, sensitive and imaginative mind. The right hand may have a straighter Line of Head. This combination shows that basic creative urges can be utilized in a structured way.

Politicians also need the ability to put on a good performance so they would benefit from a developed Mount and a longish Finger of Jupiter ♃, and a Finger of Mercury ☿ with a long upper phalange. A politician's hand might also have a branch rising from the Line of Fate towards the Mount of Jupiter. The start of the Line of Life may have a Line of Ambition, which is a branch rising from the beginning of the line, heading purposefully for the Mount of Jupiter.

Priests and other religious leaders are also performers, as they have to stand in front of a congregation. They are likely to have a well-defined Mount and long Finger of Jupiter ♃. The Finger of Mercury ☿ tends to be strong and to have a long top phalange, which is often pointed, indicating a sensitive and aesthetic way of thinking and communicating.

Performers who are involved in more physical art forms, such as non-classical dancers, gymnasts and acrobats, are likely to have spatulate hands and fingers. Spatulate types always enjoy physical movement, finding a strong element of freedom and creative self-expression through the body. This does not apply to all dancers, however. The ballet dancer, for example, is more likely to have fingers that are conic and flexible; the Finger and Mount of Jupiter ♃ will still be pronounced and the Mounts of the Moon ☽ and Venus ♀ will not be flat.

The Finger of the Sun ☉ is sometimes long on the hand of an actor. This is often the case when the Finger of Jupiter ♃ is short in relation to the other fingers. An 'introverted extrovert' might have these features: someone who is rather shy deep down and lacking in self-confidence, but has managed to overcome such feelings through positive creative urges. Such a person is also likely to have a flexible palm with a bouncy, resilient surface and a good Line of the Sun.

Comedians, mimics and those with a natural and infectious humour, will have a little bump like a pimple on the tip of the Finger of Mercury ☿. This always indicates a sense of fun, especially if the Finger of the Sun ☉ is spatulate. When the space between the Lines of Heart and Head is wide, humour will be even more forthcoming. One of the best ways of holding an audience is to make them laugh.

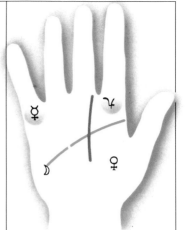

Above. A lawyer's hand. Actors and lawyers often have similar palms. Although the two professions have fundamental differences, both involve putting on a performance. Some lawyers win cases because they are such brilliant, persuasive actors and communicators when they perform in court.

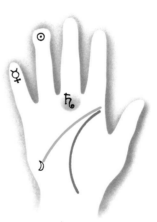

Above. This is the palm of a 'dramatic' person with a highly coloured attitude to life. He or she may not be on the stage, but will often be in the throes of some personal drama. The Line of Head plummets towards the bottom of the Mount of the Moon ☽, revealing a dramatic way of thinking. The Finger of the Sun ☉ has a very wide tip, showing creative ability. The Mount of Saturn ♄ is high, so there is also a serious side to the personality.

	Line of Affection		Line of Heart
	Line of Fate		Line of Life
	Line of Head		Line of the Sun

A WAY WITH WORDS

'There is a book in everyone', as the saying goes, implying that we all have the ability to express ourselves through the written word. This is not strictly true, but it is surprising how many people do enjoy writing, be it a diary, journal or letters. Many people write poetry, especially when young; and budding authors all over the world are at this very moment filling paper with their ideas, feelings and thoughts.

A way with words can also refer to talent with the spoken word. The power of oratory is of prime importance in many professions, such as politics, religion, teaching, law and drama to name a few. If the Finger of Mercury ☿ is long in relation to the other fingers and the top phalange is longer than the two below, gifts of eloquence and fine oratory are indicated (see top right). If the long tip is also pointed, the owner will be able to use verbal talents in an amusing way.

The power of speech is not always used constructively, however. A glib, persuasive person may also possess these features on the Finger of Mercury ☿, but the finger is likely to lean towards that of the Sun ☉ as well. Generally, the straighter the Finger of Mercury, the more straightforward the thinking via word or deed.

When the top phalange of the Finger of Mercury ☿ is long *and* has a bulbous look and a developed pad (see middle right), the eloquent owner will be full of ideas. Note the Fingers of Jupiter ♃ and the Sun ☉. If they are long, together with a long, bulbous top Mercury phalange, this will show a person with the confidence to put ideas into effect, probably through oratory skills, bringing the ability to sell inventions and commodities.

A fork at the end of the Line of Head is often found on the hand of writers, especially when the line terminates below the Mount of the Sun ☉ and slopes towards the Mount of the Moon ☽ (see bottom right). This is known as the 'Writer's Fork'. Other factors need to be present, however, to denote actual literary talent. Creative ability is usually accompanied by a Line of the Sun of some kind (see page 55, top). When there are several of these lines towards the top of the hand, many creative ideas are likely, though it may be difficult to focus energies in one direction. Constructive,

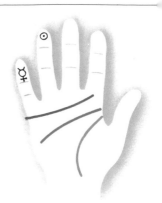

Above. This palm shows a Finger of Mercury ☿ with a long top phalange. The owner will be mentally active with a strong urge to talk or write.

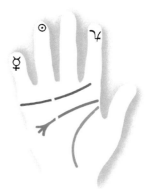

Above. A bulbous tip to the Finger of Mercury ☿ shows someone bursting with ideas. The edge of the palm curves outwards beneath Mercury, revealing a restless mind.

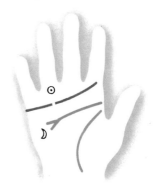

Above. This hand, which shows a 'Writer's Fork' on a Line of Head that terminates under the Mount of the Sun ☉, has quite short fingers in relation to the length of palm. Here thinking will be quick and intuitive.

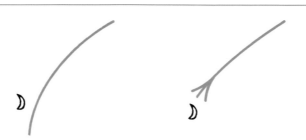

Above. Inspiration will be erratic and spasmodic for someone with an undulating Line of Head.

Above. A dramatic response to life and a powerful imagination, as shown in this very sloping Line of Head, can help the creative writer.

Above. A three-pronged fork, or trident, on a Line of Head that slopes gently towards the Mount of the Moon ☽ can sometimes denote brilliance.

conscious channelling may be necessary.

A very wide fork at the end of the Line of Head can indicate a strong sense of drama and theatrical self-expression through the written or spoken word. A small trident or three-pronged fork at the end of the Line of Head is a very good sign as it can reveal adaptable mental abilities.

Take into account the Line of Head on both hands. If the one on the left hand shows a steep dip towards the Mount of the Moon ☽ whilst the one on the right runs a straighter course across the palm and ends in a small fork, the basic thinking will be very imaginative. In time, the owner of such may be able to formulate ideas and express the imagination through writing.

An imaginative Line of Head and eloquent Finger of Mercury ☿ on a soft, malleable hand can belong to a person who may dream of writing, but never actually get down to doing it.

Anyone attempting to write will need to be confident about his or her ideas. Look at the Mount of Jupiter ♃. If it is neither flat nor too high (in relation to the other mounts) it shows confidence. If the mount is very developed, the owner may be overtly self-certain and like to blast ideas at others, bludgeoning them with words – written or spoken – in a bombastic way.

Square-tipped fingers can help one to organize ideas. A sense of order is very important for the writer, especially for those writing informative, practical works as opposed to creative genres.

The urge to release and express oneself through the written word can be arduous. A fairly full upper thumb can help the someone with creative writing talent to find the physical energies and re-sources necessary to 'stick at it'. A firm – but not too stiff and unyielding – thumb indicates deter-mination and staying power.

If you think you might have some writing talent, a good exercise is to record your everyday observations and thoughts, then put what you have written away for at least six weeks. On read-ing it again you will soon realize your mistakes, or be surprised by your budding writing talents.

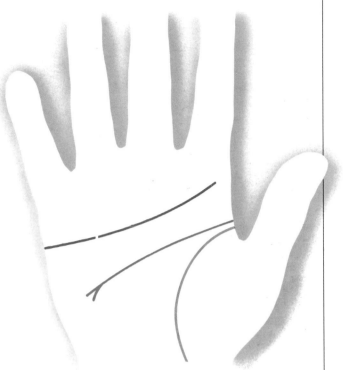

Above. This hand has a 'Writer's Fork' together with a Line of the Sun, which rises from the Line of Head and touches the fork. This shows the ability to use one's ideas in a creative way.

Below. This person has a way with words but is not creative. The 'Writer's Fork' rises towards Mercury ☿, so words will be used in practical ways. Note the straight, rational Line of Head.

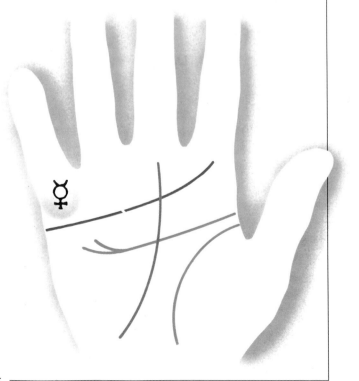

Line of Affection	Line of Heart
Line of Fate	Line of Life
Line of Head	Line of the Sun

THE INVENTIVE HAND

The human race has evolved through its ability to come up with new ways of doing things and improving existing inventions. 'Necessity is the mother of invention', as they say. Most of us have some innovatory skills, which often come to light when there is a problem to be solved. Some people, however, are particularly talented in this way.

Inventive people often have spatulate fingers, revealing their original ways of thinking and doing things. A square palm with spatulate fingers (see top left) indicates that original ideas could be used in practical ways. This sort of hand could belong to the 'do-it-yourself' enthusiast who enjoys turning his or her hand to most things that need to be done around the home.

A hand with very knotty joints on the fingers (see bottom left) reveals that the owner is likely to be a very careful thinker, putting ideas into practice only when every detail has been worked out thoroughly. The square finger-tips (except for that of the Finger of Mercury ☿) show patience and a busi-ness-like attitude towards new ideas. The Line of Head has a creative slope to it, showing a good imagination. The full Mount of Mercury means that

Above. This spatulate-fingered hand belongs to a busy, in-novative person who is tactile and original. Such an active type may need a special place, such as a workshop or study, in which to feel free to explore possibilities. Space could be a major requirement for this sort of personality.

Above. Inventors sometimes have knotty joints, which means that they are very deep, analytical thinkers. Such hands can be good at carrying out intricate tasks, which can be useful for someone invent-ing practical things. These fingers are short, promoting quickness and dexterity, which may balance the need to think everything through in detail.

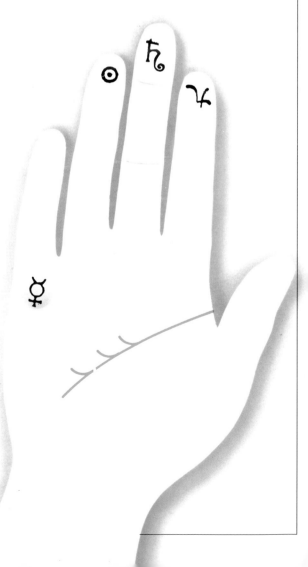

Right. This is the hand of a potentially highly creative in-ventor, who will use abilities well. When the Finger of Saturn ♄ has a long middle phalange, a love of science and an investigative mind is likely. The Line of Head has little lines rising from it, which can correspond with inspiration. Two of them veer towards the Finger of the Sun ☉, which will promote creative ideas. The good Line of the Sun further enhances artistic ability. Here, scientific apti-tude may be connected to the arts, such as in inventing special effects for films. The last line from the Line of Head rises towards Mercury ☿ in-dicating lucrative communica-tive skills. The defined mount helps generate ideas and creates a youthful attitude. The triangle on the Mount of the Sun at the end of its line shows that pleasure will be derived through using inven-tive ideas. The Finger of Jupiter ♃ is quite short, but the lack of confidence that this can reveal will be greatly negated by the strong Line and Finger of the Sun.

ideas will always be forthcoming. The pointed Finger of Mercury and knotty joints mean that they will be painstakingly thought out; some of them could be very clever, though a tendency to over-analyse tiny details could delay them being put into practice.

The Line of Head can reveal a great deal about the way a person thinks. The quality of the line shows mental strengths or weaknesses, powers of concentration and imagination. The illustration (see right) shows a long, gently sloping Line of Head. Generally speaking, the longer the Line of Head, the more intelligent the person. A well-defined line adds strength and concentration. In between the Lines of Head and Heart, there is a cross. This is called the Cross of Intuition and would help an inventive thinker to come up with new ideas (see Psychic and Intuitive Signs, pages 68-69). This cross can bring psychic gifts, but will not necessarily correspond with an interest in psychic phenomena. It gives the ability to just 'know', often in a flash, how a new idea can work. Though linked to the thinking processes, this cross works independently to logic and can be a source of sudden sparks of original ideas for an inventive person. A combination of intelligence, intuition and a scientific turn of mind, together with a high Mount of Mercury ☿ and a good Line of the Sun could belong to a person with wonderful inventive abilities. A firm hand and strong thumb will help ensure there is determination to put ideas into practice.

Whenever you see a Line of the Sun rising from the Line of Head, any success will have come about through use of one's own, not other people's, ideas. This is because the Line of Head represents thinking, while the Line of the Sun is connected to creativity, possible success and, to some extent, sensitivity to the environment. When a Line of Sun emanates from the Line of Head, thinking and ideas can therefore be realized in a creative or even successful way.

You may come across a palm with two branches from the Line of Head (see above right), one branch curving towards, perhaps touching, but not entering, the Mount of the Moon ☽ and another rising to the Mount of the Sun ☉. The branch to the Moon means that imagination can

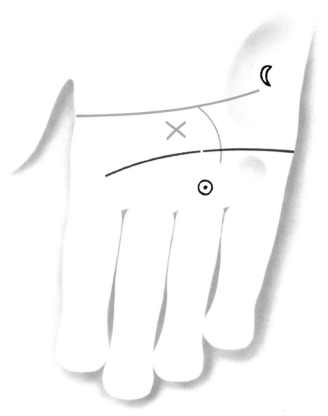

	Line of Affection
	Line of Fate
	Line of Head
	Line of Heart
	Line of Life
	Line of the Sun

Below. Several features combine here to reveal the hand of the eternal inventor, whose mind is constantly waxing and waning with ideas.

be quite ingenious and there will be a constant flow of ideas. The branch to the Sun often corresponds with creativity. The owner will have the ability to visualize well and to see, in the mind's eye, a finished picture of the current idea before it begins to be a reality. New ideas and plans will constantly surge up in the imagination. Sometimes, however, this can create impatience with any task in hand, and bring the temptation to rush off and begin something new, leaving other things unfinished.

If you feel you have thought of something innovative that could be realistically marketable, then why not try to do something with it? Keep the idea to yourself until you have protected it with a patent or copyright. Then try to sell it. Many inventions are created by ordinary people. One really good idea could change your life.

DESIGNS ON STRUCTURE

Many people are able to think in structural or even three-dimensional ways, sometimes without being aware of it. Creative ability of any sort will usually correspond with a Line of the Sun. A person with a feeling for design, shape and form is likely to have this line, be it short or long.

Those with the ability to paint and draw, depicting images in two dimensions, have different hands to those whose skills are linked with design and structure. Conic or spatulate hands are often those of the artist whose creativity is visual, but people with structural abilities, particularly architects, are likely to have square fingers or a hand with mixed fingertips. If the latter is the case, the Finger of Saturn ♄ is highly likely to have a square tip.

There are many people who utilize their creative skills in practical ways: the keen and creative do-it-yourself person, for example, may be remarkably skilled at building and creating a home environment in original ways and even making the things within it. Here you would be likely to find a square palm and fingers and a Line of the Sun. Such people often have careers far removed from their creative hobby, and there may be a lack of ambition beyond what is done to, or in the immediate environment. Some of these industrious, talented types make a far better job of what they do there than many professionals.

Have you ever started to make something and not finished it? Lots of people go on to something else before finishing a project. Short-fingered people can become impatient with doing things that take a long time to complete. If the Line of Head slopes, the ability to visualize the finished article can be so strong that the urge to finalize a project physically can wane easily. If this applies to you, it may be a good idea to give your unfinished inspirations to someone with more patience and perhaps less vision than yourself, in preference to just throwing them away. Use your abilities to create things that can be made quickly.

When examining creative hands, do not forget

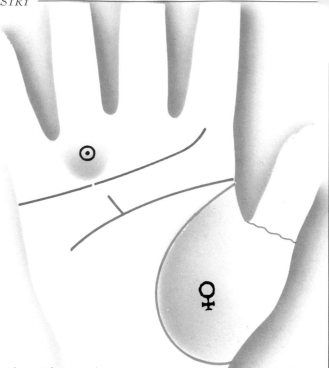

Above. The Family Ring is found between the base of the thumb and the Mount of Venus ♀. When it appears on a round, soft hand with a sloping, imaginative Line of Head, a long, caring Line of Heart and a good Line and Mount of the Sun ☉, it could provide inspiration for making useful things for loved ones.

Below. An architect is likely to have square palms, reflecting a practical disposition, and good Lines of Fate and the Sun. The Mount of Mercury ☿, which helps the organization of ideas, will probably be developed, as will the Mount of Saturn ♄, which shows an ability for design of a structural, practical nature.

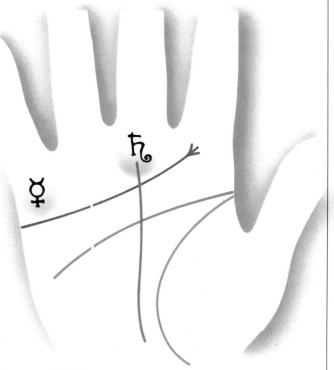

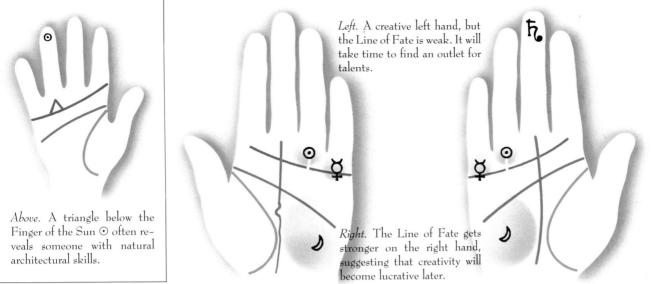

Above. A triangle below the Finger of the Sun ☉ often reveals someone with natural architectural skills.

Left. A creative left hand, but the Line of Fate is weak. It will take time to find an outlet for talents.

Right. The Line of Fate gets stronger on the right hand, suggesting that creativity will become lucrative later.

to look at both the right and the left hand. From the left hand, you will be able to discover the basic tendencies and how creative talents have been used in the past. The right hand will tell you how these skills will be developed in the future.

Look at the two larger hands illustrated on this page (see above right). They belong to John, who designs domestic appliances for a living. At first glance, John's two palms look quite similar. His Lines of Life and Head are *not* joined at the beginning, indicating spontaneity. The Mounts of Mercury ☿ and the Sun ☉ are developed and close to each other, signifying that ideas and creativity respectively combine well. The Line of the Sun is good, stemming from the Line of Head, showing talents that come from one's own ideas. The Mount of the Moon ☽ is developed, furthering creative vision.

The Lines of Fate show change. On the left hand, this line is rather weak, but much stronger on the right hand. This suggests that John found his spontaneous creativity somewhat difficult to put to practical use in early life. Later, however, he realizes a stronger sense of purpose and is able to use his skill to forge a successful career. The strong line comes into effect around the thirty-third year, bringing patience and staying power.

John's Finger of Saturn ♄ has a square tip on his right hand. This feature always shows structural, creative skills. As it is found on the right hand only, it suggests that further enhancement of his basic creative ability will come in the future.

Note the Line of the Sun emanating from the Line of Head. This indicates that success for John will be realized in his mid-thirties; and by that time, his tendency to be a bit moody — indicated by the developed Mounts of the Moon ☽ — will be a less powerful factor in his personality. Such mounts can be a fount of great imagination but like the moon can ebb and flow. The square Finger of Saturn ♄ on the right hand, however, promotes stability and structural ability.

The strong Line of Fate on the right hand stands well away from the Line of Life, whilst on the left, the Line of Fate curves towards the Line of Life. This shows that family concerns, which would not actually interfere with or delay career matters as such, would demand some time and attention, albeit temporarily.

John's palms reveal that his feeling for form and design could be put to good use, though his impulsive disposition would be suited to projects that do not take too long to complete.

We often unconsciously practise an ability to create pleasing forms in our lives and especially in our environment. We arrange our furniture and other belongings in ways that please us. Our aesthetic senses can be developed in various ways through interior decoration, especially in our choice of colours, shape and form.

Line of Affection		Line of Heart
Line of Fate		Line of Life
Line of Head		Line of the Sun

ASSESSING ACADEMIC ABILITY

There are several features of the hands, palms and fingers that reveal a lot about academic abilities and teaching skills. The most important line on the palm in relation to the intellect is, as you may expect, the Line of Head. Generally, the longer the Line of Head the more intelligence there is. There are other factors to take into account as well.

When looking at the hand to assess academic ability, remember to examine both hands. Many people take up intellectual pursuits later in life; if this is, or is to be, the case, the right hand's Line of Head will be longer than that of the left, as the mind reaches out to absorb more information. Sometimes the left hand has a very sloping Line of Head, whilst that of the right is straighter. This indicates that the mind will be used in a more practical way as time goes by, and that creative thinking can help to bring inspired interest to rational thinking.

The quality of the Line of Head is important in assessing academic ability. The line should ideally be fine and clean-cut. If it is broad and heavily etched into the palm, the intellectual ability will still be good if the line is long, but

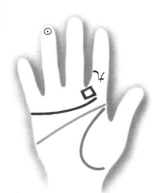

Above. A square on the Mount of Jupiter ♃ can signify teaching skills. These need not apply only to teaching in the academic sense, but may correspond to a general ability to pass on useful information.

Above. Triangles are pleasing but islands are not. When appearing on the hand of a student, islands can indicate mental strain. If tiny hair lines descend from an island, they show worry and stress.

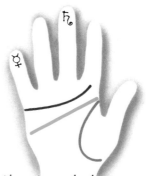

Above. A straight, heavy Line of Head suggests that the thinking will be unimaginative, especially if this line is similar on both palms. If the fingers and thumb are stiff and unyielding, a rather dogmatic attitude is likely.

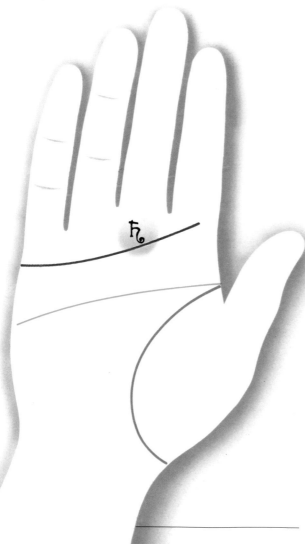

Left. Here is a long Line of Head that almost reaches the edge of the palm. This would certainly belong to someone with a powerful mind. The line is also clearly defined, fine and clean-cut rather than coarse and wide. In conjunction with a long Line of Head, these features suggest that the power of the intellect is strong, the memory good and the thinking processes well organized. The Line of Head runs parallel to the Line of Heart, creating a neat quadrangle between the two lines, indicating balanced and reasonably broad-minded attitudes. The developed Mount of Saturn ♄ further enhances serious intellectual ability and helps concentration for long periods.

	Line of Affection
	Line of Fate
	Line of Head
	Line of Heart
	Line of Life
	Line of the Sun

will not be so finely attuned or sensitive.

When a person is acquiring new intellectual skills, little triangles are often found on the Line of Head. Triangles always correspond to pleasing influences and are often linked to learning. Their position on the Line of Head can reveal the actual subject or point of interest. If they are found beneath the Mount of Saturn ♄, there can be a deep interest in history; when found under the Mount of the Sun ☉, the arts may be a source of great pleasure; when they are found just beneath the Mount of Mercury ☿, language or other forms of communication may be a current interest.

Some academics are not necessarily clever but are the owners of really good memories. They can register information in their mental filing cabinets and are able to regurgitate it well, thereby seeming brighter than they actually are. A long but very straight Line of Head often belongs to a person who thinks a lot, but in rather unoriginal, boring and practical ways. Such a tendency will be marked if the space between the Lines of Head and Heart is narrow.

A fork at the end of the Line of Head is an excellent sign, but the smaller and neater the better. This donates balance and cleverness and often is found on the hands of those with literary talents. If the fork is wider (see right), the mind will sparkle with intelligence, but concentration may be short-lived and there can be a tendency not to finish things as the mind tends to float off in a new direction after the initial flare of interest has died down.

The Finger of Mercury ☿ is linked to thinking and communicative ability. An academic who writes or teaches would therefore possess a strong Finger of Mercury with a long upper phalange. If the mind is very busy with ideas, the fingertip will be full. If the thinking is heavily ponderous and serious there may be a heavy tip to the Finger of Saturn ♄.

Teachers generally have a good Line of Head and a longish Finger of the Sun ☉, which can contribute to a love of children. They often have a small square on the Mount of Jupiter ♃ (see page 60, top right) and the Line of Heart tends to be straight. These features can enhance aptitude in and enjoyment of teaching.

Above. If the Line of Head is more deeply cut into the palm than the Line of Heart, the mind will rule the head and emotions will either not register deeply or will be heavily analysed intellectually.

Below. This wide-forked termination to the Line of Head often belongs to people with brilliant and natural academic abilities, whose spontaneous intelligence can be diluted and rendered less effective through the strictures of a highly disciplined education.

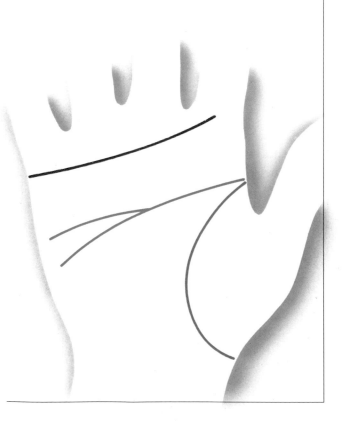

THE OUTDOOR TYPE

Are you the outdoor type? Perhaps you like gardening, bird-watching, walking or sailing. We all need to get out of our stifling cities and be in touch with nature as often as we can. The great outdoors does not appeal to everyone: many people are happy with a small garden or nearby park. Many lines and features on the hand can reveal a person's attitude to nature and need for open spaces.

People who actually live from and in the countryside, such as farmers and horticulturists, often have square hands and fingers, sometimes with small thumbs. The second phalange of the Finger of Saturn ♄ may be longer than the other two, especially on the hands of those interested in more scientific aspects of agriculture or horticulture. People with 'green fingers' often have square hands and a rather flat look to the overall palm, with perhaps the exception of the Mount of Venus ♀, especially where there is a love of flowers and gardens.

Those who work in a manual capacity on the

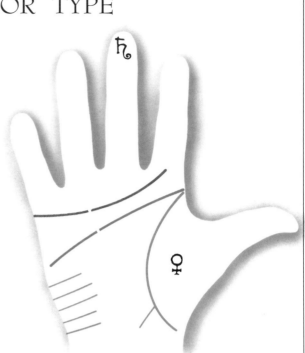

Above. A sharp fork at the end of the Line of Life shows a restless personality. He or she will need to travel but will also enjoy returning home after a long trip.

land are likely to have elementary hands. They may not greatly appreciate nature in an aesthetic sense, but if they had to change and work in an indoor environment their soul would suffer.

A square tip to the Finger of Jupiter ♃ can indicate a love of large landscapes and scenery; if there is artistic ability, the owner of such will love going off to try to depict the landscape through painting or drawing, to frame or capture a beautiful scene.

Very wide palms often indicate an expansive disposition that dislikes feeling physically restricted by small, stuffy buildings. Spatulate fingers will underline this tendency. Activity will be very important to such a person; the wider the scope for exploration the happier this type is.

Many outdoor types enjoy travelling. A branch curving away from the end of the Line of Life towards the Mount of the Moon ☽ is a Line of Travel (see left). The owner of such a line will enjoy exploration and travel; if the Mount of the Moon is developed, the need to commune with

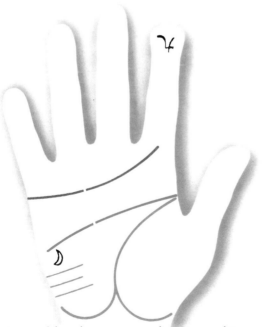

Above. A powerful need to get away is shown by a Line of Travel curving towards the Mount of the Moon ☽. The spatulate Finger of Jupiter ♃ suggests that the owner enjoys physical contact with nature.

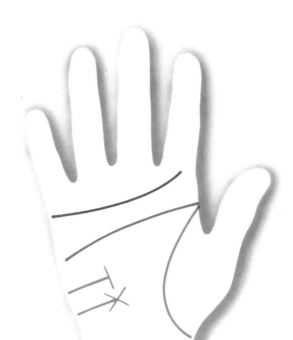

nature without company or distractions can be enjoyed. A partner of someone with this need will have to exercise understanding and let the other go off without too much fuss because to deny this sense of freedom could create big problems.

We all need fresh air and exercise, and many of us enjoy keeping fit. Sportspeople often have wide-tipped fingers and men tend to have hairy hands. In both sexes, the back of the hand has coarse skin and the palms tend to be rather dry. For some people, however, fitness becomes an obsession. Outdoor types who feel unfulfilled unless they put the body through a punishing regime can create problems. Moderation, as always, is the key to a healthy life-style.

———— Line of Affection	———— Line of Heart
———— Line of Fate	———— Line of Life
———— Line of Head	Line of the Sun

Above. A Line of Travel with a crossbar over it can mean a fear of going to far-away places, or it can correspond with a specific fear, such as flying or the sea. A cross on a Line of Travel means that an intended journey could be accident-prone; whilst the cross remains on the line it would be a good idea to postpone travelling. Small marks, like crosses, come and go.

Below. Some athletes possess a combination of the Lines of Heart and Head, known as the Simian Line (see pages 90-91). Found on any hand, this rather unusual line reveals an intense side to the personality. If this line is found on the hand of someone with an interest in sport, and the hand is strong and sinewy, there can be a love of intense, demanding competitive activity, such as running and cycling.

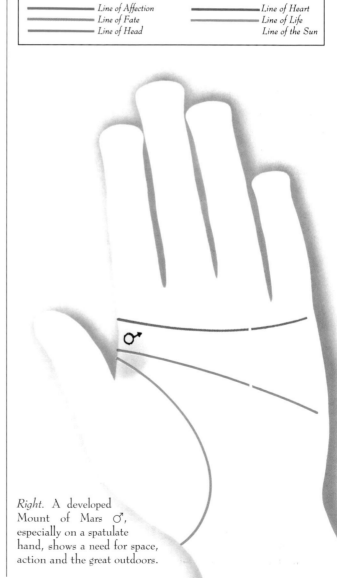

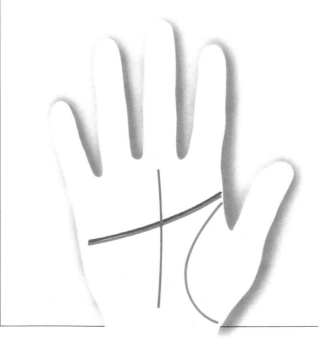

Right. A developed Mount of Mars ♂, especially on a spatulate hand, shows a need for space, action and the great outdoors.

THE SCIENTIFIC HAND

Every day, new discoveries are made. We live in very exciting times in terms of scientific developments. In the past few decades, humankind has taken enormous steps that have changed the planet, but not always for the better. Hopefully, discoveries yet to be made will enable us to put right some of the damage done, or find effective means of dealing with damage that is irrevocable. In a way, we have opened a Pandora's box through

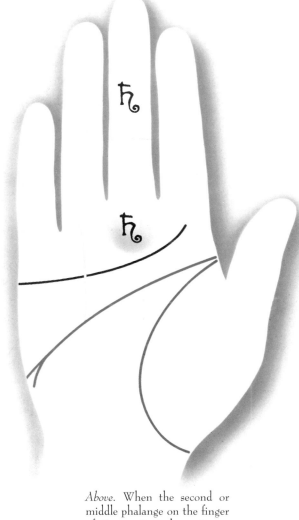

Above. When the second or middle phalange on the finger of Saturn ♄ is long, it can denote a love of serious scientific research. Subjects such as physics, chemistry and pure mathematics are likely to be a source of deep interest to the owner of such a hand.

our scientific discoveries and unleashed into the world elements that we do not know how to handle. Now we have to endeavour to catch up with ourselves.

The scientific hand is likely to have a good Line of Head that is long and clearly marked. If this is the most defined line on the hand, especially if the Line of Life is the most finely etched, the scientist could be an 'absent-minded professor' type: very cerebral and rather detached from the physical world, often neglecting bodily needs. Scientists tend to have long fingers. These will be as long as, or even longer than, the palm itself and indicate great interest in the mental, as opposed to the physical aspects of life. The fingers are also likely to be firm and moderately flexible.

There are many branches of science, so it follows that there are all sorts of scientists with all manner of hands, discovering, testing, analysing and changing our world. The Line of Head, however, may indicate the main line of interest. You have learned that the more sloping the Line of Head, the more imagination there will be. In some areas of science, intelligence will unite with imagination to explore, understand and explain what is discovered. In such cases, the Line of Head will be strong, clear and sloping.

If the Mount of Saturn ♄ is developed and found in conjunction with a long middle phalange on the Finger of Saturn, the scientist may be terribly serious in his or her quests and may also have to shoulder a lot of responsibility. There will be a need to be alone to think and work, but not too often, for too much isolation could result in a rather melancholic stance. If a good Line of the Sun is also found, it will help to lighten the personality. On the illustration (see left) it grows from the Line of Head, indicating possible success, or at the very least, much pleasure, in utilizing one's own ideas in a positive way. The long Line of Head slopes, showing imagination. The line is very well defined with a small fork at its end, which will promote the ability to document findings in written reports and theses.

Knotty joints correspond with an analytical

turn of mind. A hand with such joints is one of the five basic types and is known as the 'philosophic' hand (see Significance of Shape, page 13). Knotty joints reveal serious thinking, reflection, attention to detail and sometimes fussiness. These attributes can be very useful in scientific work, which often requires patience and intense concentration.

There are three areas on the fingers where knots may be found. The meanings of the knots are influenced by the position in which they are located. If present on the joint between the top and middle phalange, they indicate a great concern for detail, which can sometimes be extreme. Such a tendency may be beneficial to someone working in scientific research, but not when applied to other situations or people. The distrust these particular knots signify can also denote a reserved attitude towards anything new. Analysis, rather than discovery and development, would therefore be the most suitable area of scientific work for this type.

Knots found on the joint between the middle and lower phalange have a very different meaning. A precise, orderly and clear way of thinking and an ability to store a lot of information in the memory will enable a scientist to work in a very constructive way. This type often seems impractical when it comes to normal, everyday activities. He or she is sometimes rather untidy in appearance and lives quite happily in a chaotic environment. This is because the mind is so busily caught up in intellectual meanderings that the external, physical world takes second place. To other people, this type of scientist may seem vague and distant. They may have problems relating to and communicating with people on a more mundane level. You can imagine the archtetypal 'mad scientist' pondering on the birth of the universe oblivious to the soup stain on his trousers.

Knots directly below the finger-nail are fairly uncommon. Again, they denote a particular type of scientific mind. They tend to belong to very logical people who are able to apply their thinking in useful ways. A scientist with these knots may be very good at finding new ways of doing things, or improving existing methods. Not as original in thought as the 'mad scientist' described above, this type would be better suited to using theories and ideas that have been discovered by others.

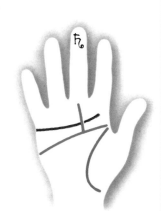

Above. A branch rises, straight and clear, from the Line of Head towards Saturn ♄. This can indicate a vocation for science and will promote a serious belief in what is done.

Above. When there is a square tip to the Finger of Jupiter ♃, there can be an interest in the natural world. This is often found on the hands of scientists who study natural history.

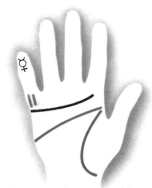

Above. Two short, vertical lines on the Mount of Mercury ☿ can indicate a love of science and an ability to understand abstract subjects, such as mathematics.

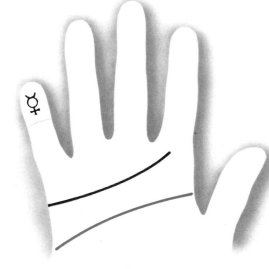

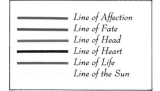

Left. A knot on the Finger of Mercury ☿ between the top joint and the beginning of the finger-nail, together with a long, straight Line of Head, will enable a scientist to work in practical ways and can promote concentration. Chemistry or forensic science may suit this type.

———	*Line of Affection*
———	*Line of Fate*
———	*Line of Head*
———	*Line of Heart*
———	*Line of Life*
———	*Line of the Sun*

HEALERS AND HELPERS

The urge to heal comes from the heart. Many people are potential healers without being aware of their power. There is a special mark on the hand, made up of tiny, vertical lines, which is rather grandly known as the Healing Stigmata. It is found above the Line of Heart and below the Finger of Mercury ☿ (see below). People who spend most of their time caring for others, such as spiritual healers and those in the medical professions, are likely to have these little lines. People who are kind, sympathetic and able to be a 'good Samaritan' with genuine concern for others, are also likely to have the Healing Stigmata. In addition, the hand of a healer should be soft and have a good, springy feeling. A palm with a hard texture can literally indicate a hard disposition.

Be careful not to confuse the Healing Stigmata with the lines that represent children (see Will You Have Children?, pages 86-87). Lines of Children are found above or very close to the Line or Lines of Affection. Other, similar little lines can also be found in this area, which are not concerned with healing: they have a rather scratchy look and are reddish in colour and can indicate the presence of gum disease or infection.

A healer will have a sympathetic and empathic disposition, which is likely to be reflected in a long and clear Line of Heart, which gently curves towards the Mount of Jupiter ♃ to end somewhere on the middle of the mount (see below right). The Mounts of Venus ♀ and the Moon ☽ will not be flat and the overall colour of the palm will not be too pale or red.

The Finger of Jupiter ♃ is linked to faith and sometimes to religious belief. If it has a conic tip (see below right), it adds to idealistic and intuitive

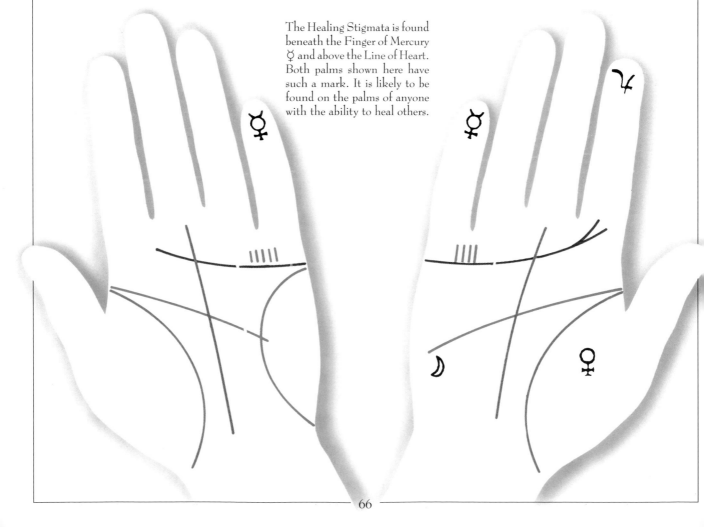

The Healing Stigmata is found beneath the Finger of Mercury ☿ and above the Line of Heart. Both palms shown here have such a mark. It is likely to be found on the palms of anyone with the ability to heal others.

ability, which are essential qualities for a healer.

The space between the Lines of Heart and Head is called the quadrangle (see right). This area can reveal much about a person's mental attitudes. If you are not actually reading a hand, but just catch a brief glimpse of it, you can find out if the owner is likely to have a talent for healing.

A person practising metaphysical healing will have a broad-minded attitude and an imagination that can be applied constructively. The quadrangle on the palm of such a person is likely to be wide. The illustration (see right) shows both a wide and a narrow quadrangle. If the space between the Lines of Head and Heart is narrow, it literally corresponds with narrow attitudes, as if there is not enough space in the quadrangle to allow wider ideas to be accepted. If the space is very narrow, a sense of humour may be lacking, especially if it is narrowest under the Mount of Saturn ♄. Healers often have a marvellous sense of fun. Laughter is the best medicine of all.

The Mount of the Sun ☉, when developed, is associated with our innermost abilities and potential. When found on the hand of a healer, it can help to radiate warmth and positive energies, especially when it leans slightly towards the Mount of Mercury ☿ (see right).

The fingers, as you have learned, reveal a lot about a person's attitudes. A person with the ability to reach out towards others will have flexible fingers, with fingertips that bend away from the palm easily. The thumb will have a balanced look and will not be too stiff. It is likely to have a 'waist', showing diplomacy and tolerance.

The Cross of Intuition, found in the quadrangle, indicates intuitive thinking (see right). Another, rather more unusual line, is the Line of Intuition. It is often crescent shaped and curves up the palm from the Mount of the Moon ☽ towards the Finger of Mercury ☿. When found on the hand of someone who would like to be, or who is a healer, this is an excellent mark, as it enhances one's ability to be in touch with psychic energies stemming from the unconscious.

———	Line of Affection	———	Line of Heart
———	Line of Fate	———	Line of Life
———	Line of Head		Line of the Sun

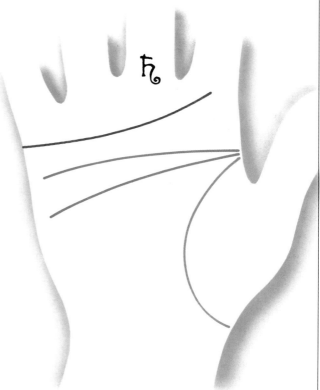

Above. The space between the Lines of Heart and Head is known as the quadrangle. Two Lines of Head are shown on this palm to demonstrate the difference between a wide and a narrow quadrangle.

Below. The Cross of Intuition is found between the Lines of Heart and Head. The Line of Intuition curves from the Mount of the Moon ☽ to the Finger of Mercury ☿. Healers often have both these marks, as intuition greatly enhances their abilities.

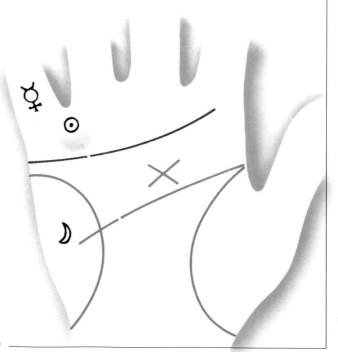

Psychic and intuitive signs

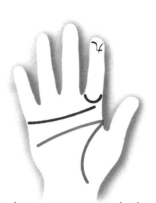

Above. Quite a rare mark, the Ring of Solomon is a semi-circle around the base of the Finger of Jupiter ♃. It can donate a deep interest in the occult and bring commitment and talent in psychic matters.

Above. The Cross of Intuition is found on the hands of people with psychic and intuitive ability. Three positions in which it can be found are shown here.

Above. The Line of Intuition runs from the base of the Mount of the Moon ☽ in a semi-circle towards the Mount of Mercury ☿. As the Cross of Intuition is also found on this palm, there will be strong psychic gifts.

Perhaps you are psychic or very intuitive without realizing it. Do you ever think of someone and the next moment the phone rings and it is that person? How often, after a special event in your life, do you realize that you 'knew' it was going to happen all along? Around 85 per cent of women and 45 per cent of men are very intuitive or psychic.

Many people regard psychic ability with fear, preferring to ignore the information that can filter through from the unconscious. They stubbornly refuse to believe in anything that cannot be explained rationally.

In the past, millions of people were put to death in Europe because the Church deemed them to be witches. This reign of ignorance and cruelty that destroyed so many innocent people has contributed to certain fears that still exist today, as there is still an echo of the terror our forefathers knew. On the other hand, there are those amongst us who are so enamoured by anything that is 'psychic', they will not make a single decision without consulting a clairvoyant. Such misplaced faith often leads to a lot of money being wasted. A clairvoyant worth his or her salt will always tell people to make their own decisions, will not encourage dependence, will give advice and guidance but never make profound statements that annihilate decision-making, for everybody is ultimately responsible for their own actions.

The Cross of Intuition, or 'la croix mystique', is a mark found on the palms of many very intuitive people. It can donate a natural gift for the occult and mysticism. Situated in the quadrangle (the area between the Lines of Head and Heart), this mark brings the ability to think intuitively. It has nothing to do with intelligence or logic, but is linked to quite a different area

Above. On a psychic's hand, the Mount of the Moon ☽ will sometimes have a deeper, pinker colour than the rest of the palm, indicating an active inner world. A well-developed mount can bring vivid dreams and visions.

of the mind. It can bring a knack of just 'knowing' and can be very useful in all aspects of life, as well as the psychic realms.

The Cross of Intuition is usually to be found in the centre of the quadrangle, but can be situated anywhere within it. When it is located close to the base of the Mount of Jupiter ♃, occult studies or practices may be employed in ways that feed self-aggrandisement. If it is found under the Finger of Saturn ♄ or is formed by crossing over the Line of Fate, it means there is a serious attitude towards religious matters and a need to adhere to truth, accompanied by an urge to study, research or perhaps teach, often in subjects linked to the occult or mysticism. There can also be a talent for writing about such. If the cross is found near to the Mount of the Moon ☽, occult leanings will be tinged with a certain amount of supersititon, or a tendency to enjoy the more sensational aspects of psychic areas, but not usually in a harmful way. Close to the Moon, this cross can promote the ability to influence others and can bring success, particularly in mysticism, and sometimes in metaphysics, poetry or painting.

Some of us are easily able to 'plug into' our intuitive faculty, but for many it is not so straightforward, even though the ability is there. It often comes in a flash, divorced from rational thought. We are often so geared to working things out in a logical manner that when something comes to us irrationally through the gift of intuition we can lose it. The rational mind will want to have its way and can in effect create doubt about whatever has been perceived intuitively. To encourage this gift, try not to lose the lightning flash of an understanding or an idea by thinking too much about it. If you know deep down that you have intuition, then use it. It is often difficult to trust something that cannot be logically explained, but do not worry about that. Perhaps if we learn how to trust and better utilize aspects of our unconscious, including the intuitive and psychic areas of our beings, we will open the doors of our perceptions and discover more power to influence our lives positively than we ever dreamed of.

Interest in various aspects of metaphysics is booming. There are many groups and organizations that are actively involved in development of psychic skills. If you really want to learn you will be able to find others who share your interest and who can teach you, but do be careful. You should avoid certain occult groups that want to charge you a lot of money for showing you how to develop psychically. Be wary too of those who employ sensational, theatrical methods of going about things. There are a lot of charlatans and other unpleasant types who have no integrity and who may use their psychic abilities to further their own ends.

To learn how to use your abilities safely, you will need an experienced teacher who will help you to develop your potential with care. He or she will not only help you to 'open up' but will also teach you how to protect yourself on a psychic level as there are negative as well as positive areas in your subconscious. As you open up its doors, you could be vulnerable. It is a good idea, therefore, to seek a good teacher who will know how to gently and safely guide you and ensure you come to no harm. As you learn to read palms, you may find that your own psychic abilities come to the fore, but bear in mind that this usually takes time and try to be patient.

	Line of Affection		Line of Heart
	Line of Fate		Line of Life
	Line of Head		Line of the Sun

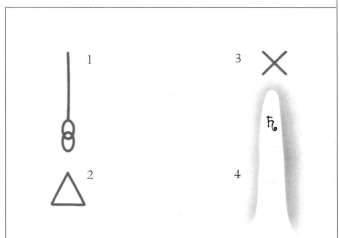

Above. 1. A figure 8 at the beginning of the Line of Fate can donate premonitions. 2. A triangle under the Finger of Saturn ♄ can bring special psychic powers. 3. A cross on the Mount of Saturn can mean psychic powers may be used to make a living. 4. A long upper phalange on the Finger of Saturn can increase psychic perception.

Sophie's hand (life-size)

SAMPLE READING
SOPHIE'S HAND

This is the left hand of a right-handed woman writer. Remember that the left hand shows basic tendencies and past events. The hand is complex, with many unusual features. Before examining the lines, the fingers are very revealing. The fingertips are conic, which often corresponds with creativity and sensitivity. A propensity to think deeply is revealed by the long fingers.

The Line of Head is particularly interesting as it forms two distinct branches. One plummets down to the lower portion of the Mount of the Moon, whilst the other ends higher up on the palm, towards its outer edge. The upper branch of the Line of Head ends in a wide fork, which is often linked to writing ability. The lower one slopes deeply, showing that Sophie is very much in touch with her imagination and subconscious factors. The wide 'writer's fork' also creates dramatic thinking, and can make any harsh conditions extremely difficult to cope with. Note that from the early part of the Line of Head fine little lines rise towards the Mount of Saturn, telling that there were indeed severe and unhappy conditions to deal with. The lower branch of her Line of Head rendered her a dreamy and very sensitive child, with an inner world full of vivid dreams and fantasies. Sophie developed severe asthma at the age of seven, which meant she had little regular school attendance and formal education. As a result, she retreated further into her inner world. She read a lot and wrote poetry.

Although Sophie's palm, particularly her Line of Head, is highly creative, there is no Line of Fate on this palm. On the right hand, however, (not shown) her Line of Fate is very clear and strong and her Line of Head slopes gently without branching. If she had the same Line of Head on both palms, she would not have been able to put her imagination to productive, practical use. A Line of Fate on the right, but not on the left palm, indicates that a defined feeling of purpose

and direction came to Sophie a little later than to most people.

The Finger of Jupiter is long, reaching more than half-way up the top phalange of the Finger of Saturn, indicating confidence. This has further enabled Sophie eventually to use her talents. Although the palm looks confusing at first, examine it carefully and you will be able to see a fine and clear Line of the Sun. It rises from the upper fork of her Line of Head, revealing her creative thinking. Despite her early difficulties, this line helped to provide her with a positive outlook and the capacity for happiness.

Look at the inside of the Line of Life and you will see another line running alongside on the Mount of Venus. This is the Line of Mars. It acts as a protective influence and brings strength and resilience. In Sophie's case, it indicates that, though there was illness and unhappiness, there is also some resilience, an inner source of strength that has enabled her to feel less vulnerable.

The Girdle of Venus, together with the long and defined Line of Heart, show an impassioned, perhaps rather extreme, response to life. This also furthers Sophie's creative inspirations, however, as she experiences life through her emotions in a powerful way. Note also the Cross of Intuition in her quadrangle, showing her intuitive, and possibly psychic, ability.

At the time of writing, Sophie is in her mid-forties and has written a very successful book. The Lines of Fate and the Sun on her right hand have become well-defined and promise great achievement and happiness. In summary this left hand reveals unusual talents, a very problematic start in life, but also an underlying confidence which has served Sophie well. She will always be basically rather difficult to understand, very sensitive and rather dramatic. But all these factors have combined well in her to culminate in original ideas and the gift of writing.

COMMON QUESTIONS

1. My hobby is writing short stories, but no one has seen them. Does my hand show writing ability?
Your fine, forked Line of Head and good Line of the Sun show talent, though your short Finger of Jupiter ♃ reveals a lack of confidence. The triangle on your Line of the Sun can mean success. Be brave. Approach some publishers.

2. Everybody tells me their problems. I am good at helping people sort out their lives. Could I be a counsellor?
You have a Cross of Intuition, a good Line of Heart and a long, intelligent Line of Head. The quadrangle is wide, indicating broad-mindedness. See what openings are available in terms of training.

3. I am learning to play the piano. Could I ever be good enough to be a concert pianist?
Your developed Mounts of the Moon ☽ and Saturn ♄ show that you are musical. Keep practising.

4. I am at drama school and love character parts. Could I be successful?
The branch from your Line of Head to Jupiter ♃ shows ambition and ability for acting and mimicry.

5. I love photography, but can only afford a cheap camera. I feel this limits me. What should I do?
Your sloping Line of Head and good Line of the Sun show creativity. Your developed Mount of the Moon ☽ shows imagination and your full Mount of Mercury ☿ reveals that you are observant and lively. Carry on.

6. I am female, beautiful and seventeen. Will I fulfil my dream to become a famous film star?
You do not have a Line of the Sun, which usually accompanies fame and creativity. As you are young, however, the line may yet develop. Your long Line of Head denotes intelligence, so other areas of your life may be successful. Enjoy your beauty and use your good mind.

7. I am fascinated by physics. Although I have had little formal education, I have enroled for evening classes. Is this a good idea?
Your long Line of Head, a mark beneath your Finger of Mercury ☿ and the long middle phalange of the Finger of Saturn ♄ can be good for sciences. Work hard.

8. My father is a lawyer and wants me to be one too, although what I really want to do is travel. What would be my best move?
A dominant personality is needed to be a lawyer. This is often indicated by a long Finger of Jupiter ♃. As yours is short, however, law may not be your forte. Lines of Travel show that you will go abroad.

9. I have studied the tarot for three years and would like to do readings professionally. Is this a good idea?
You have a Cross of Intuition in your quadrangle and a good Line of Intuition circling your Mount of the Moon ☽. Try it.

10. I feel I have no special talent. I used to love making clothes, but now cannot be bothered. Will this change?
Your sloping Line of Head shows creativity, but the little hair lines drooping from it show temporary depression. As these disappear, you will become more enthusiastic.

11. My husband does not want me to go back to college and I am bored being a housewife. What should I do?
Your long, clear Line of Head shows that you are intelligent and that your brain needs stimulus. Your Line of Affection forks at the end, and there are little hair lines drooping from it. This indicates minor problems. Be tactful with your husband, but do your own thing.

12. The line that represents my fourteen-year-old son is long and shows potential success. He is lazy, however. How can I make him ambitious?
Do not push him. The fact that the line is so long shows that he will forge his own purpose well. This will be sooner rather than later if you let him be.

13. I paint in my spare time. A friend wants to exhibit my work in his gallery. I am worried in case I am a failure. Should I refuse?
The long tie between your Lines of Head and Life indicates a lack of confidence, but a star on the Mount of Jupiter ♃ indicates success. Accept this opportunity.

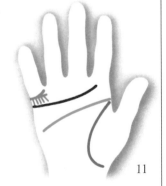

14. I create many computer games, but recently I feel as if I cannot think clearly or get my ideas together.
An island on your Line of Head may mean that your mind has been overworking. Have a break.

15. I am retiring soon and want to do something creative. Pottery appeals. Should I buy a wheel?
Your Line of the Sun begins high on your palm showing that, in later life, you will find pleasure and contentment in creative pursuits. Pottery sounds like a good place to start.

16. I prefer my own company, writing poems and reading a lot. My mother says I am too insular and antisocial. Should I make an effort to change?
The circle at the base of your Finger of Saturn ♄ shows that you enjoy solitary activities. Be yourself. Perhaps your mother is lonely.

Line of Affection	Line of Heart
Line of Fate	Line of Life
Line of Head	Line of the Sun

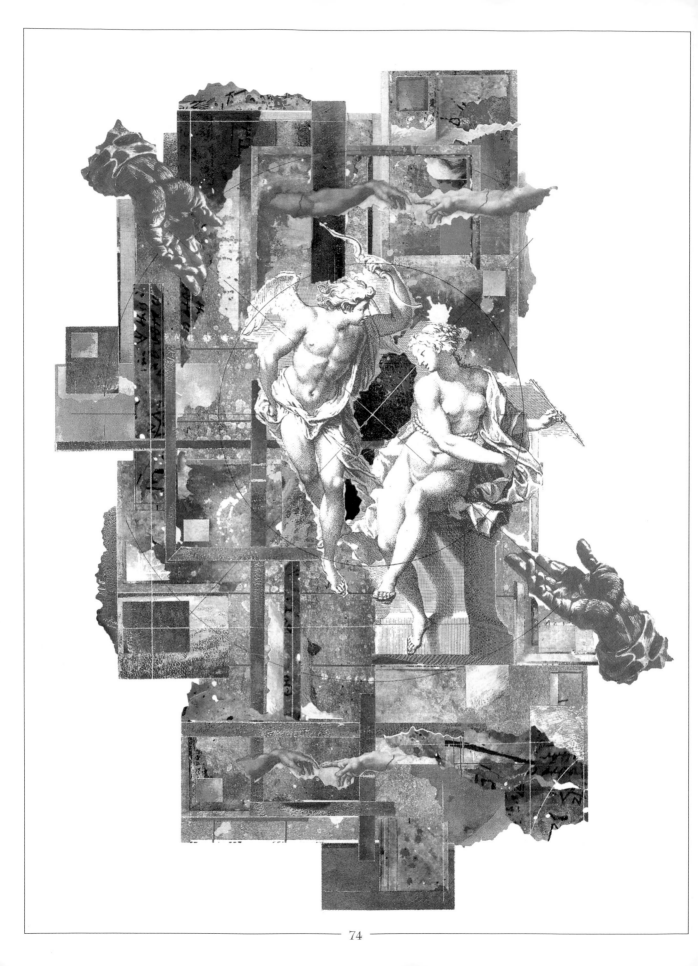

Chapter Four

LOVE AND RELATIONSHIPS

Love is the most important aspect of life for us all. Human love can manifest in many different ways, be it physical, spiritual or a meeting of minds. However it is experienced, it means closeness, understanding and sharing.

In this chapter, you will learn to read the Lines of Affection. Also known as the Lines of Marriage or Relationship, they reveal our past, present and future loves. They do not always correspond with marriage or the equivalent, but can be found whenever there is a close bond between two people. The lines that indicate children sometimes correspond with a couple's cherished ideas.

There are many ways in which love may blossom or fade. At some point in our lives, most of us experience unrequited passions, the pain of separation or rejection. All these emotions will be mirrored on the palm, as will one's attitude towards romance and sexuality.

We often think of love only in terms of close relationships, but our finest feelings may radiate through compassion, kindness and generosity. Any powerful emotion for another will be echoed in the hand.

LOVE AND HAPPINESS

The two main ingredients that contribute to happiness are love and work, but love comes first. We all need love. All of us have it within us to give and receive, but the complexities of human nature can render love and the pursuit of happiness the most difficult aspect of life. Love is the crown of a myriad of emotions.

Although we all have the capacity for love, some of us are blessed with a more inherent ability to express and realize it than others. Emotional difficulties, especially experienced in our formative years, can distort a loving heart or render happiness elusive in adult life. The hand and the lines on the palm can reveal how much we can love, how we are likely to be loved in return and when, during the course of our lives, we are most likely to find and experience true happiness.

The Line of Heart is especially relevant in showing how loving we can be. Generally speaking, the longer the line, the more affection will be felt. A good line will terminate around the middle of the Mound of Jupiter ♃, indicating a kind and loving person who can let feelings of love pour forth easily. Tiny branches rising from such a good Line of Heart towards the fingers promote a sense of realism. If they are absent, there can be too much self-sacrifice and idealism, and a tendency to fall in love rather too easily and maybe too often.

Two branches rising from the Line of Heart, one ending under the Finger of Saturn ♄, the other beneath Jupiter ♃, can tell of luck in love, and possibly of a very fulfilling partnership. They can also denote achievement in other areas of life, which may come about through having a positive, warm, likeable disposition.

If the Line of Heart is very long, it can create problems. However, the deeper and more defined the Line of Heart is the better. As the heart is the mirror of emotion, the owner of a strong line, especially one terminating beneath Jupiter ♃, will be emotionally strong. The organ itself will have a corresponding fortitude. The sex drive will be healthy, particularly if the line is pink and not paler than the others on the palm.

A Line of Heart that is very thin compared to the others with no branches rising from it can reveal that matters of the heart are not a major factor in life. This is particularly the case when the line falls short of the Mount of Jupiter ♃. If you imagine the Line of Heart to be a conductor of loving feelings, the thin line literally means that loving others will not be a prime factor. A self-centred nature is also likely, with the owner of such a line not needing or responding much towards others in terms of realizing happiness.

When the Line of Heart sends a line up towards the Mount of the Sun ☉, it can donate a very happy relationship, which will bring joy and good things. When you are looking for signs of happiness on a hand, take into account the hand as a whole. Remember that a Line of the Sun of any length will always contribute to a positive disposition, that the Line of Head can show mental attitudes and that the quadrangle between the Lines of Head and Heart reveals humour when it is not too narrow. A sense of fun will always be advan-

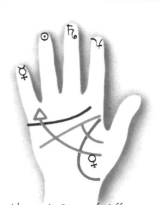

Above. A Line of Affection crossing the palm to the Mount of Mercury ☿ and ending in a triangle shows a love affair that culminates in a happy union.

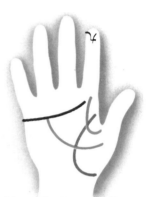

Above. If a Line of Affection stops at the Line of Heart, it can mean the loved one is not completely free and may even be already married.

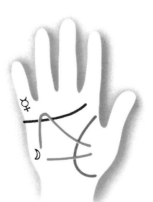

Above. A happy relationship with a foreigner can be shown in a Line of Affection moving out towards the Mount of the Moon ☽.

tageous and can promote happiness in any situation. The Mount of Venus ♀ is also linked with love. A full mount contributes to feelings of love and especially passion, desire and sensuality.

Love and happiness extends far beyond romantic relationships and can mean many things to many people. Some people love animals more than humans, others may be in love with money, power or themselves. A happy period in life, affecting the emotions positively, will register on the lines of the palm in various ways.

Main emotional ties are usually indicated by the horizontal lines under the Finger of Mercury ☿. Other relationships, including love affairs, however, are to be found in lines on the Mount of Venus ♀. These lines can cross the Line of Life and veer towards the mount of Mercury as an affair begins to flower (see top left). In either position, these lines are known as Lines of Affection.

Terminating beneath the Line of Head (see middle left), a Line of Affection can reveal a love that is somehow prevented by the ideas of others: a difference in religious belief, for example, could create parental disapproval thwarting a union, though 'f the love was strong enough, it would find a way to continue, and the line would move beyond the Line of Head.

A Line of Affection rising to the Mount of Jupiter ♃ (see middle left) can indicate a happy union with someone successful. Sometimes it can also suggest an ambitious attitude towards marriage, such as a desire to marry 'well'.

When a person changes his or her mind about a committed, established relationship and chooses, happily, to break it off, you may find a Line of Affection going up towards the Mount of Mercury ☿ and then dipping down to the Mount of the Moon ☽ (see bottom left).

The centre of the palm can reveal a lot about the ability to realize happiness and fulfilment in life. If you find that the left palm has a defined dip in the middle, it can suggest that the owner has felt disappointed with his or her emotional opportunities in life. He or she may literally feel empty and dissatisfied. This may be justified when life has been full of major disappointments, but some people have an attitude that is not able to acknowledge happy influences readily. If, however, the right hand does not have a concave centre, then, as life goes on, it will feel better, fuller and happier.

Emotional satisfaction can also be found beyond the personal sphere. Many people are naturally full of joy and compassion and want to share these feelings with others. Such a person is likely to have a pink palm, with soft skin and a bouncy feeling. The Mounts of the Moon ☽ and Venus ♀ would be developed, but not too much.

When pleasure is found through humanitarian love, a life of celibacy is sometimes chosen. On the palm of such a person, any Line of Affection found beneath the Finger of Mercury ☿ is likely to turn upwards at its end. When a person experiences a period of time without a partner, there may be a corresponding space on the Mount of Venus ♀ devoid of horizontal Lines of Affection.

———— Line of Affection		▬▬▬ Line of Heart
———— Line of Fate		———— Line of Life
———— Line of Head		Line of the Sun

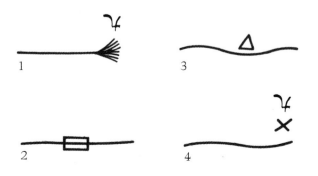

Right. 1. When the Line of Heart ends in a little fan on the Mount of Jupiter ♃ it means that a person has an intrinsically happy, loving disposition and is likely to realize harmonious relationships. 2. A square on the Line of Heart signifies a stabilizing, helpful factor that may modify any emotional crisis.

Left. 3. Triangles always reveal pleasing times. On the Line of Heart, they indicate happiness and good feelings. 4. Crosses on the palm do not usually have happy connotations, but when a clear cross is found on the Mount of Jupiter ♃ it can mean a very happy period, relationship or marriage.

THE FICKLE HEART

A fickle heart – an emotional disposition that is inconstant, uncertain, capricious or perhaps fearful of commitment – can be revealed on the hand in several ways.

A person with a fickle heart may be just a flirt, always attracted in a light-hearted way to the opposite sex, without actually having love affairs. He or she may indulge in many fantasies, which may be harmless enough. If such a person is married or in a close relationship, however, problems are highly likely. Even though you may be lucky enough to be in an ongoing and happy relationship, it is very likely that, unless you are a saint, there will be times when you find yourself very attracted to another. But do you do anything about it? Do you succumb to what is probably going to be a fleeting fancy? Are you easily flattered by the attentions of an attractive stranger? If you want to leap into a brief affair, are you able to lie and deceive your partner? Many people do, and if there is a predisposition towards being fickle, your hand is likely to reflect it.

Generally speaking, people with square hands and fingers tend to be reserved and somewhat cautious. They may not, therefore, be easily inclined to

Above. A wavy Line of Heart can literally correspond with a changeable emotional disposition and an inability to know what is wanted in a relationship. This type can 'blow hot and cold', say one thing and then do something else. In extreme cases, they promise all sorts of things one day and have a change of heart the next. If this sort of line is found only on the left hand, there will eventually be a more settled attitude to life.

Above. A chained Line of Heart, particularly on a soft hand, reveals responses that are too easygoing or a rather lazy emotional disposition, which lacks moral strength and discernment. If the fingertips are round, these tendencies may be amplified. A continuous, chained line sometimes means the heart itself is under strain or lacks energy for some reason. If there is lassitude and fatigue, it would be wise to seek medical advice.

Right. This Line of Heart is crossed by many short lines, showing numerous fleeting attractions. The Lines of Affection reveal several partners early in life. The feathery Line of Heart eventually settles and a more constant Line of Affection can be seen, showing that emotional stability will come later and bring fulfilment. Note on the Mount of Venus ♀ the upper part has several small lines running inside the Line of Life, further indicating earlier emotional inconsistency. If these factors are found on a very flexible hand that also has wide spaces between the roots of the fingers, the combination could further an ability lightly to pick up and let go again of a current passing fancy.

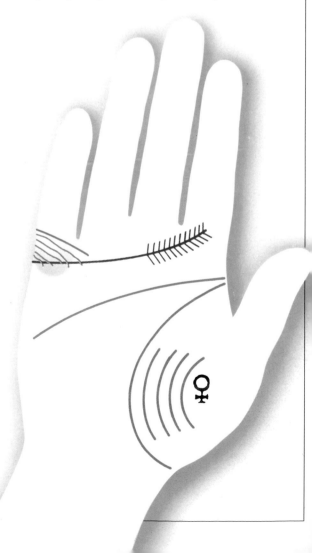

	Line of Affection
	Line of Fate
	Line of Head
	Line of Heart
	Line of Life
	Line of the Sun

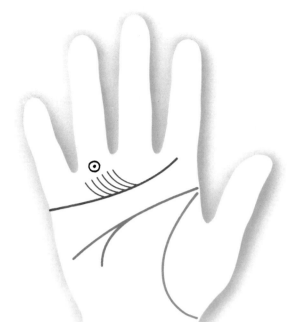

Left. A very wide gap between the Lines of Head and Life reveals the spontaneous disposition of someone who will often rush at things with little regard for the consequences. The Line of Heart has lots of little hair lines pointing to the Mount of the Sun ☉, indicating a tendency to idealize love affairs. The 'glamour' of romance can be very appealing and there may be a tendency to be unrealistic, to feel bathed in the light of some current romantic attraction. The Line of Head slopes, showing imagination, which, in this case will further the unrealistic image of the object of desire.

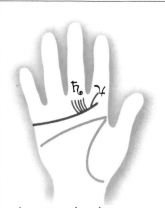

Above. Tiny hair lines rising from the Line of Heart towards the Mount of Saturn ♄ can reveal a changeable, turbulent emotional life, with many doubts, uncertainties and fears. There could be unsatisfactory relationships, which would eventually give way to more peace and happiness. This Line of Heart is long and sends a line branching up to the Mount of Jupiter ♃, indicating pride in matters of affection. Loved ones may be set on too high a pedestal.

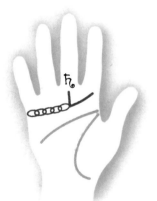

Above. A broad, deeply cut Line of Heart with chains as far as the Mount of Saturn ♄ can indicate feelings of uncertainty, or even dislike towards the opposite sex. A fickle heart in this case may tend to play on the feelings of those who respond to advances. This person could enjoy using the other, not just for personal or sexual gratification, but to satisfy their own rather destructive feelings.

impetuous, rash behaviour in matters of the heart or otherwise. This trait is underlined when the fingers are inflexible and bunch together tightly.

Conic-fingered people can be easily influenced, especially if the fingers are flexible and have spaces between them at their roots where they join the palm. It is not true that such hands always reveal an inconstant heart, but the naturally outgoing and friendly disposition will respond to others with far less reserve than the square and practical type.

Spatulate-fingered hands often belong to those who do not respond well to conventions. Although they enjoy exercising their originality, they are often constant and true in relationships. There are, of course, exceptions. The need for freedom of expression may include an urge for sexual liberty, but there can be innate common sense that curbs such desires.

Hands with very pointed fingers often belong to the romantics and the idealists of this world. If the top phalanges are very long and pointed, idealism will be marked. Such a person may tend to fall in love with the idea of love. The fickle heart here may be more in the mind than in the body.

Soft lights and sweet music may not thrill one with elementary hands as much as the other types. Instinct links with desire and powerful feelings can often manifest through lust in love.

The philosophic hand belongs to those of an analytical disposition, especially when the lower joints of the fingers are developed. When there is also a short Line of Heart, caution, reserve and a tendency to analyse everything in detail may create an over-fussy emotional response. Any inclination to be fickle-hearted may be negated and romantic ripples may not extend beyond the convoluted mind.

Remember when reading the hand of an older person that although the body ages, the heart often does not. A flirtatious person may always be on the look-out for a little romance. Clouded, fading, ageing eyes can still look through a veil of romantic fantasy. We are never too old for love.

THE PASSIONATE LOVER

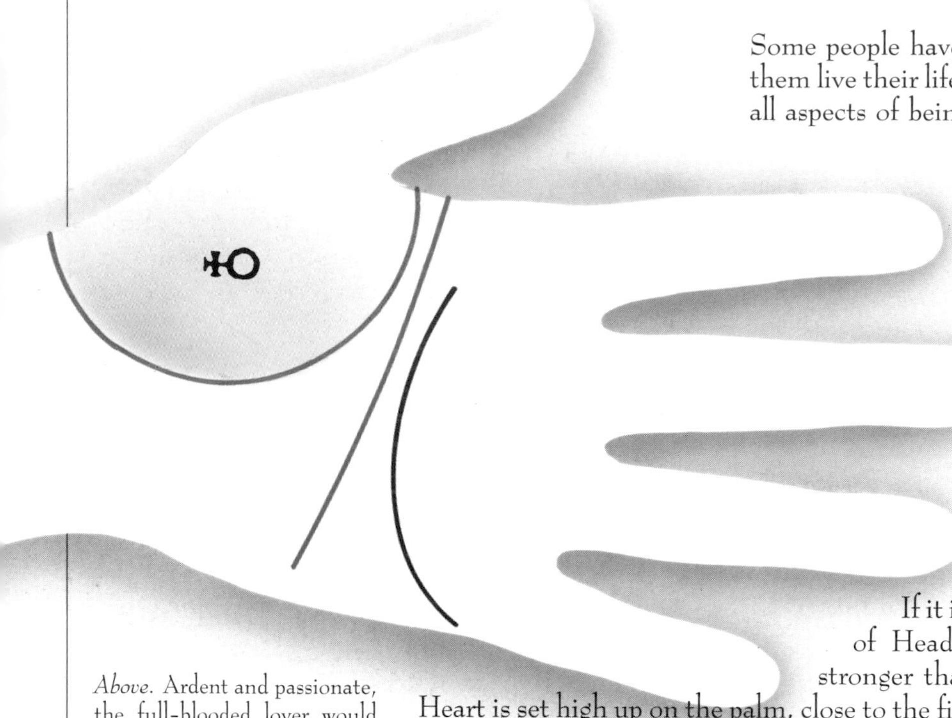

Some people have a passionate nature, which makes them live their life in a full-blooded way, experiencing all aspects of being with depth, colour and intensity. For such people, love affairs can be especially powerful.

Passion can manifest in several ways on the hand, particularly on the Line of Heart and the Mount of Venus ♀. The passionate lover, in the physical sense, is likely to have a full Mount of Venus and a Line of Heart that is low on the hand (see left). Generally, the lower the Line of Heart, the important the sensual side of love will be. If it is very low, almost touching the Line of Head, then passion and desire will be stronger than reasoning ability. If the Line of Heart is set high up on the palm, close to the fingers, the love nature will tend to be more idealistic and cerebral. If the Mount of Venus is very full and high and has a redder colour than the rest of the palm, combined with a coarse-looking hand with chunky fingers and few lines on the palm, sensuality is likely to be a strong factor in the personality.

The Girdle of Venus (see below) is like a secondary Line of Heart (see The Artistic Hand, pages 50-51 and The Broken Heart, pages 92-93). It is a semi-circle often found rising from the area between the Fingers of Jupiter ♃ and Saturn ♄, ending between the Fingers of the Sun ☉ and Mercury ☿. This line is not present on all hands and can vary in its length and uniformity. Where it exists, it helps to deepen emotional and sexual responses and can add extra spark to life generally, and can be particularly beneficial to those involved in creative work or appreciation. The Girdle of Venus shown here dips down and links with the Line of Heart. This indicates that the passionate side of nature can be difficult to handle and that lust and desire will need to be controlled. Sexual needs will dominate the emotions. This trait will be underlined even more if the Mount of Venus ♀ is very developed.

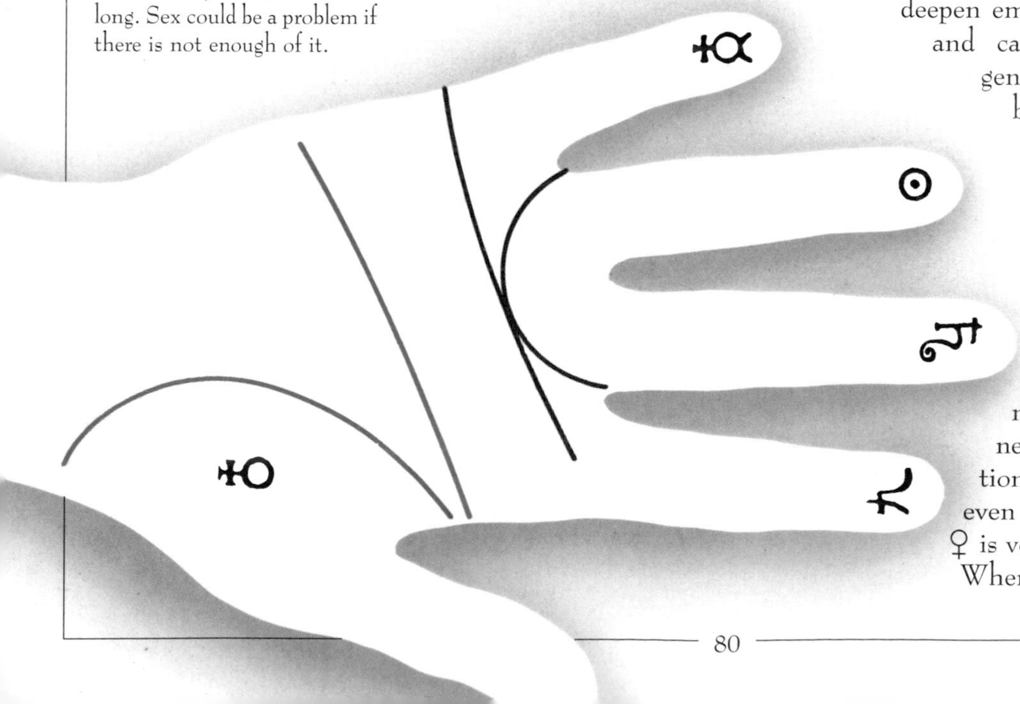

When passions run high, it is not

Above. Ardent and passionate, the full-blooded lover would have a developed Mount of Venus ♀ and a low Line of Heart. He or she would need, and probably get, lots of physical action.

Below. The Girdle of Venus shows rather over-the-top sensuality. This person might not be easily sated, or not for long. Sex could be a problem if there is not enough of it.

unusual for the 'green-eyed monster' of jealousy to rear its head. If the Line of Heart is very long, it can reveal a possessive and jealous disposition. Such feelings may extend beyond the actual relationship and apply to everything else in which a lover is involved, such as his or her family, job or anything else that divides the attention of the lover. If the Line of Heart does not extend to the edge of the palm but ends on the Mount of Jupiter ♃, it is a good sign, meaning that the emotional life will be rich and varied.

A long Line of Heart, together with a sloping, imaginative Line of Head, means that jealous feelings could get out of perspective. The imagination could run riot, fantasizing about what a loved one may be doing. If the Finger of Jupiter ♃ is short, then irrational jealousy would be linked to insecurity and some basic lack of confidence.

The Simian Line (see A Law Unto Themselves, pages 90-91), where the Lines of Head and Heart combine, can often correspond with an impassioned disposition. This is a relatively unusual line. Simian types are always intense in some way, although this is not necessarily a negative trait. When it comes to passion, feelings can get out of perspective because emotional reactions can swamp and overwhelm reasoning. Such people need understanding partners.

The hands of people from warmer countries tend to have higher Mounts of Venus ♀ than those from colder climes. We often associate northern people with a reserved, even cold nature that reflects their climate. Similarly, people from warmer, southern countries tend to be thought of as more demonstrative and emotional. This often applies particularly to people from the Mediterranean countries of southern Europe, whose natures tend to be more impassioned and heated.

Above. A long Line of Heart that terminates at the edge of the hand reveals jealousy.

Above. Jealousy could get out of control when the Line of Head slopes steeply.

Above. A short Line of Heart ending beneath the Mount of Saturn ♄, together with a full Mount of Venus ♀, suggests a love nature that is more sensual and passionate than idealistic. This is especially so if the hand or Mount of Venus is rather red and the Line of Life is strong and well-defined. There could be strength and determination in pursuing desires, but not much sentimentality or romance. Some men with hands like this can be rather selfish in their sexual responses and insensitive to the finer feelings of those who love them.

Below. A straight Line of Heart tends to cool down passion. If the rest of the hand has sensual indications, the love nature may be strong in the physical sense, but feelings from the heart may be rather remote.

Line of Affection	
Line of Fate	
Line of Head	
Line of Heart	
Line of Life	
Line of the Sun	

Below. This curved, longish Line of Heart is a very positive sign. It shows a need for love to be as important as sex. Someone with such a line is likely to have a warm, caring and emotional disposition.

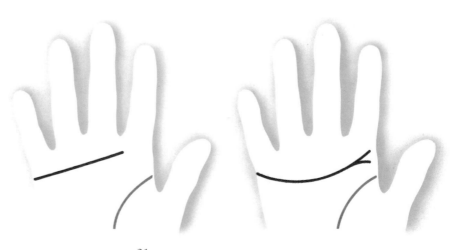

THE HANDS AND COMPATIBILITY

Opposites attract. Two people with different qualities can bring balance and complementary elements to a relationship. Sometimes people are attracted to each other because they have a similar personality and outlook on life. They will initially be able to communicate from the same stance, like two plants in the same garden. There may not, however, be enough friction to spark the flames of active growth and development to further a lasting relationship. Either or both could feel stuck, static and root-bound in the common ground that at first seemed so comfortable.

Opposites can also repel, or differ so much that there is no foundation on which a relationship can grow and flourish. A person totally different to oneself can be fascinating, but when it comes to living together, the qualities that seemed so riveting may lose their magic, and conflicts can arise.

Here we will look at various personalities, examining what is revealed about them through the shape of their hands and what they may need in terms of a compatible relationship. On pages 84-85 in the section on Soul Mates, we will look more closely at the lines on the palm and what they have to say about compatibility.

Above. A spontaneous and extravagant disposition is revealed by several features on this hand. There are wide spaces between the fingers at their base, and there is a significant gap between the Lines of Life and Head. The Finger of the Sun ☉ is long, which means that the owner may have a reckless attitude towards money. The long lower phalange of this finger will promote a love of things, but there may also be a lack of taste, with a preference for garish and ostentatious objects to 'show off'. Such a person would need to be rich, or married to someone who can afford reckless spending and similarly lacks aesthetic sensibility. A person who could encourage some prudence would also make a good partner. Practical attitudes and realism are the domain of hands with square palms and fingers.

Below right. This is the hand of a very reserved person. There is a short Line of Heart and a long tie between the Lines of Life and Head at their beginning. See how the Line of Life does not sweep out towards the centre of the palm, but is close to the thumb, indicating a liking for what is homely and familiar. Such a person would need a partner with more of a sense of adventure and confidence, but not too much. The reserved type needs to be gently encouraged, but not overwhelmed, by such a partner. A long Finger of Jupiter ♃ would be a good feature for a potential partner to have as it brings confidence and self-assurance. He or she should be able to understand the lack of spontaneity and need for familiarity. A long Line of Heart ending under Jupiter can promote necessary kindness and acceptance.

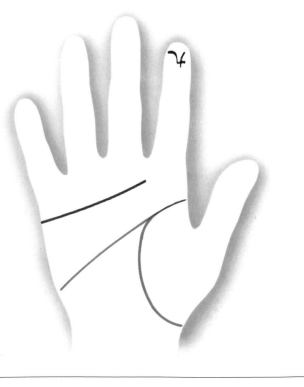

A woman with round, soft hands with tapering fingers and almond-shaped nails may be very feminine. She may have a rather superficial nature and a dependent, sometimes lazy disposition. Her appearance may be her main concern and she will need a man who can provide well for her. She is often most compatible with a square-handed man. He will be practical and business-like, and will indulge her whims. She will need to know that she can depend on him. If he has a strong Mount of Venus ♀, he will appreciate her femininity. Wide nails will help him to be patient with her and a flexible thumb creates generosity.

A man with spatulate fingers and a flexible hand will require plenty of scope to express his expansive nature. He needs plenty of activity, so would get on well with an easy-going woman with a sense of adventure. She would also benefit from the ability to create and maintain a sound home where he can relax. This sort of woman is likely to have a rounded palm with short, square fingers, which could promote the nurturing, practical qualities he needs. If her hands are inflexible and narrow, however, she may doggedly resist his attempts to encourage her to share his interests.

A person with a wide space between the Lines of Life and Head is independent and spontaneous. If a full Mount of Venus ♀ and short, round fingers are also to be seen, there will be a need to get out and about, to be gregarious and enjoy life. A partner with a long tie between the Lines of Heart and Head on stiff hands will not have such an immediate response to life and could seem dull. The more conventional, cautious type could find his or her partner disconcerting, and major problems could arise. The energy and warm response of the other would be hard to keep up with, let alone to understand.

Pointed fingers and thin, delicate hands belong to highly sensitive people. If the palm has a fine network of lines, sensitivity can be acute. A person with hands like this needs lots of understanding and gentleness. Any interactions with others, especially within close relationships, will be delicate. This type needs a partner with soft-skinned yet springy palms, signifying a combination of receptivity and strength. Hard-skinned palms can correspond with a lack of tenderness. Thoughtful, long fingers, and a strong Finger of the Sun ☉ could help a rather fragile partner feel more resilient. Practical, down-to-earth square-handed types will not suit this sort of person.

Elementary hands do not necessarily mean that the owner lacks finer feelings. Such types do, however, tend to experience life and others in simple ways, without too much thought. They are often compatible with others who have a realistic attitude, such as square-handed types. Two people with elementary hands could realize harmony through sharing the simple things in life.

Conic-fingered people, particularly those with a developed Mount of the Moon ☽, require pleasing, aesthetic influences in their environment and the people that surround them. They may enjoy the creative energy of a spatulate-handed partner, especially one involved in the arts.

Two people with inflexible, square hands and fingers may be able to get things together in practical, realistic ways, but their lives could lack excitement. They could get locked into deadening routines that affect them negatively.

The texture of the palms also reveals much about character and is worth taking into account when assessing compatibility. Generally, the softer the surface of the hand, the gentler the disposition. If the palm is very soft to the touch with little resistance to slight pressure, and the whole hand feels malleable, the owner may be very easy-going and sometimes lazy. Such a person can be quite happy to let life just 'happen' without making much effort. A relationship between two people with very soft hands could lack dynamism and action. A very soft-handed type could benefit from a relationship with someone whose palms have more resilience and bounce, and whose skin is firm, but not hard. This sort of person could inject some motivation into the relationship.

A hard-skinned person may similarly be drawn to a soft-skinned partner who could help to bring relaxing influences into the relationship. Two people with tough-skinned palms might find that their relationship gives little priority to fun.

———	*Line of Affection*	━━━	*Line of Heart*
———	*Line of Fate*	━━━	*Line of Life*
———	*Line of Head*		*Line of the Sun*

Soul mates

Love makes the world go round. In the first flush of romance, two people can spin in a heady dance of mutual excitement and discovery and feel that their bubble of love will never burst. For a while, nothing else will matter very much to them.

Inevitably, the bubble eventually pops. For some couples, its waters feed the earth in the garden of their relationship and they grow and flourish together. Others, sadly, find that their bubble has fallen on to rocky ground. The water trickles away and the couple either scratches in the dust of lost love or separates.

Palmistry can help us discover how compatible we are with a current or potential partner. We have already looked at how the shape of the palm can determine compatibility (see pages 82-83). Now let us find out how various lines on the hand can link, harmoniously or otherwise, with those of another. Here are a few examples.

A man has a feathery Line of Heart, together with many lines of influence on his Mount of Venus ♀, indicating a flirtatious disposition. His partner has a very long Line of Heart, running right across the Mount of Jupiter ♃ to end on the outside edge of her palm. This shows that she is likely to have a possessive, jealous nature. This partnership is destined for trouble, as she would be unhappy, even if her flirtatious partner does not actually have any love affairs.

A woman with a Line of Heart that ends in a little fan of lines will be very affectionate and understanding. If her partner has a short Line of Heart, terminating at the start of the Mount of Saturn ♄, he will be cooler and more

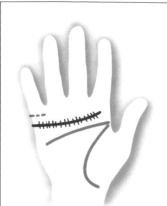

Above. Tiny spaces in a Line of Affection can mean that one's partner may often be away from home. If the line is otherwise clear of defects, such as islands, crosses or drooping hair lines, the time spent apart is likely to be due to the nature of the career, rather than emotional rifts. If the Line of Heart is fringed, there may be a tendency to be tempted by flirtations while the partner is away.

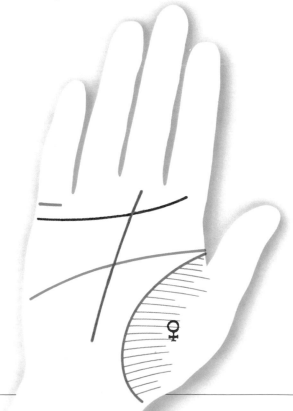

Left. Many little lines crossing the Mount of Venus ♀ often belong to people who have a lot of contact with the public. They may need to work hard to maintain an often demanding career, which requires a positive projection of the personality. Although these lines do not show romantic interactions, there will often be an element of caring for the people dealt with. A partner of such a person will need to give the other room to relax and restore energies, and provide a caring environment.

	Line of Affection
	Line of Fate
	Line of Head
	Line of Heart
	Line of Life
	Line of the Sun

Above. A very practical palm. The short Line of Heart shows a rather undemonstrative nature, the fairly straight Line of Head reveals realistic and unimaginative thinking, and the strong Line of Fate, forking up towards the Mount of Jupiter ♃, indicates ambition. Such a person will be very career-orientated and may be successful; but the absent Line of the Sun and the other factors suggest that there may not be much joy in what is achieved. Someone with a palm like this may be best suited to one who is also ambitious and very practical.

Above. Many people fall in love with someone who is married. They often waste many years hoping that the situation will change, that the loved one will leave the wife or husband, and happiness will ultimately be realized. The 'other man or woman' is like an actor's understudy standing in the wings, destined never to play the desired role. This state of affairs is very sad and more common than one may think. On this palm, a Line of Influence travels up the palm to come to a halt just below the Line of Heart. This shows that the relationship is blocked. There is just one strong Line of Affection, which dips in disappointment on to the Line of Heart. This palm could belong to someone who really loves an unavailable person and who will suffer in so doing. The Line of Heart is long and would promote an idealized image of the loved one. It could be difficult to admit that such love is wasted and to give up the fantasy. The Line of Head is very imaginative and could further colour an illusion of love. Here, fantasy is sometimes unconsciously chosen in preference to a real relationship perhaps because of some underlying fear of loss. You cannot miss what you have never really had.

practical in emotional matters, but probably reliable too. She will be so good-hearted and kind that she is likely to love him even though he may well be gruff and unromantic sometimes. She will not take his cooler nature too seriously or worry about it.

Someone with an imaginative Line of Head, sloping steeply down the palm, will need a partner who also has some, but not as much, imagination. A less-steeply sloping Line of Head is a good sign, as this will bring practical ability into the relationship without dismissing the creative imagination of either partner.

A person with an intelligent Line of Head — long, clear and gently sloping — who also has long fingers, indicating a thoughtful disposition and patience, may tend to get rather caught up in thought. If the tie between the Lines of Life and Head is long, there may be a lack of spontaneity. Such a type will certainly need a partner with a good mind, but may benefit from one who has a quicker, impulsive approach to life, indicated by a small space between the Lines of Life and Head, or a short tie between them and a springy palm. Someone with various interests for the thoughtful partner to ponder on and perhaps share would be ideal.

A sense of humour is very important in a relationship. If there is a narrow space between the Lines of Heart and Head and the tip of the Finger of Mercury $\female$ is flat, a sense of fun may not be a strong factor, especially if the skin on the palm is rather hard with an absent or very short Line of the Sun. This type would find a partner with a raucous sense of humour or a light-hearted attitude difficult to cope with.

Below. These palms belong to two people in a relationship. One partner (see left) has financial problems, indicated by the crossbars and island on the Line of the Sun. A temporary halt in the career is indicated by the broken Line of Fate. Crossbars on the Line of Head reflect anxiety. The other's hand (see right) has a good Mount of the Sun $\odot$, which will help to cheer the partner up. The Line of Heart fans out showing a loving disposition. Although both partners are worried, their Lines of Affection remain strong and true. The hand on the right also has a good Line of Mars, showing resilience.

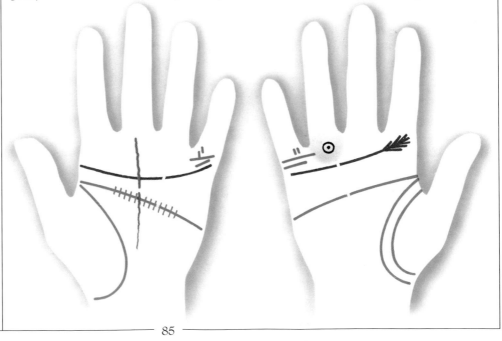

WILL YOU HAVE CHILDREN?

When a baby is born, it will already have some lines on its tiny hands, including those that reveal the children it may have when it grows up. It is sometimes possible to predict with remarkable accuracy whether or not you will have children, how many you will have and even their sex from the lines on the palm.

There are certain lines on the hand that are concerned with children. It is important to bear in mind, however, that what is revealed may not always correspond with actual offspring. A couple may share a love of their pets, for example. When two people are deeply involved with each other emotionally, they may have ideas that they both care about passionately. The fruits of their combined interests can manifest on the hands as Lines of Children.

As many people use contraception to plan their families these days, the lines depicting children can be possibilities that have not been taken up. When you are looking at hands in this regard, be careful not to raise hopes that may be false. Explain that potential children are shown on the palm and that to have them or not is mostly a matter of choice.

Although these lines can be found on the hands of both sexes, they are more usual on women's hands. However, when they do appear on a man's hands, it means that he is, or will be, very fond of his children.

The Lines of Children are finely marked, upright lines (see below left), usually found immediately above a Line of Affection. They can be very fine, so it is often a good idea to press this area of the skin gently between your fingertips to see which of these small lines stands out most clearly. It can also be useful to use a magnifying glass. The Lines of Children are read from the outer edge of the palm inwards. The one nearest to the outer edge will be the first-born.

When there are many fine lines on the area of the palm associated with children, it can have two possible meanings. A person destined to be childless who loves and works with children may feel so close to them that they will show on the hand. Beloved children of relatives can also be marked on the hand. A love of children is also revealed when the Finger of the Sun ☉ is quite long in relation to the other fingers. Many tiny lines can also indicate great fertility. In the past, when a lack of birth control meant that it was not unusual to have a very large family, each tiny line would probably have represented a child.

An adopted child can also register on the palm as a child of one's own. As adopted children are always wanted by the adoptive parents, the line representing the child can be very close to the Line of Heart.

Boys are indicated by long, broad and deep lines; shorter, fine and narrow lines show girls. The illustration (left) shows three children: two boys and a girl.

Left. Lines of Children are thin, vertical lines found immediately above the Line of Affection.

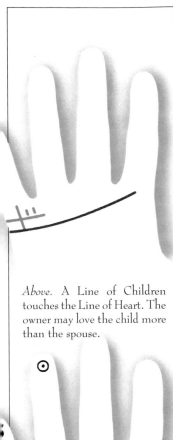

Above. A Line of Children touches the Line of Heart. The owner may love the child more than the spouse.

Above. This line travels up the Finger of Mercury ☿ showing that the child will go far in life.

When one of the Lines of Children is straight, it tells of a child who will be strong and healthy; if it is very faint, wavy or crooked, then the child may have a rather delicate constitution. A small island at the beginning of the line can mean that the baby may not be robust at birth, but will get stronger as the line becomes clear of the island.

If one of the Lines of Children touches the Line of Heart (see top left), it means that the owner of the palm may love the child more than the husband or wife. When there are two or more Lines of Children, one touching the Line of Heart can also indicate that the parent loves this child more than the others. This is particularly likely if the other Lines of Children start above the Line of Heart. If the line travels up the Finger of Mercury ☿ and is cut deeply into the palm (see middle left), it can mean that the child will go forth into the world and achieve much. If the line veers towards the Finger of the Sun ☉, it is possible that the child will be well-known.

Twins are indicated by two little lines rising from one point (see bottom left). Identical twins would show as two such lines that are exactly the same. Twins of both sexes will show in one line being darker than the other. In twins of the same sex, one is often stronger; this is revealed when one line is cut less deeply into the palm.

On the hands of parents with grown-up children, a Line of Children can 'grow' another line close to it, which represents the partner of the child. As the relationship strengthens, so will the line, especially if the parent is fond of the daughter-in-law or son-in-law. It is even possible to see grandchildren on the hand. These manifest as tiny lines close to the Line of Children.

Lines of Children that stand independently from the Lines of Heart and Affection are a good sign. Such a line suggests that the child's development will not be hindered by harmful parental influences.

If there is to be a problem conceiving a child, it can correspond with a triangular arch shape rising from the first rascette or bracelet on the wrist; or there may be a total lack of Lines of Children altogether.

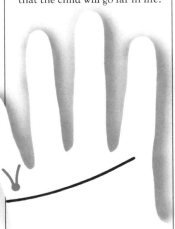

Above. Twins are shown in two Lines of Children that rise from the same point.

Below. When a person is not well-disposed towards children and definitely does not want any, this can manifest as no Lines of Children.

	Line of Affection
	Line of Fate
	Line of Head
	Line of Heart
	Line of Life
	Line of the Sun

MORE THAN ONE LOVE?

Love songs and poems wax lyrically about love lasting forever, but it is rare to find a relationship that remains constant and true and survives the tests and changes of time. The hand has various areas that reveal a great deal about affairs of the heart; here we will look at the hand in relation to more than one love.

When you are reading hands, you will often find that the main source of interest and concern will be in affairs of the heart and how they are likely to develop. As with all other aspects of palm reading, be very careful not to cause unnecessary grief. There are ways of saying things honestly without causing harm. When, for example, you see a relationship on the palm that looks as if it will not last, but that a new person will replace the present love, you can gently, and honestly, explain that the owner will be loved again. Even though the forthcoming break-up of a relationship may be painful, the knowledge that a new love is coming can help balm the hurt.

The Lines of Affection – which do not necessarily mean a marriage ceremony, but always indicate a close union – are especially relevant in finding out about affairs of the heart. They are situated under the Finger of Mercury ☿ above the Line of Heart (see top right). They are read upwards from the Line of Heart; the closer a strong Line of Affection is to this line, the earlier there will be a marriage or close relationship. Most people have at least one line here. When you find many tiny lines and one deeper and longer line, the most pronounced will correspond with the most important love in a person's life. These lines usually indicate a sexual relationship, but can sometimes reveal deep, but not physical affection. Many lines tell of many affairs of the heart and a flirtatious nature.

When there is a clandestine affair going on outside a relationship or marriage that remains undiscovered and therefore does not cause separation, it can manifest as a thinner, smaller line, very close to but remaining separate from the

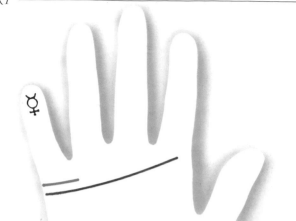

Above. The Line of Affection is best when clear and straight, with no forking at the end, and no crosses, islands or drooping lines upon it. One, clear line is quite rare, meaning a true love that will last.

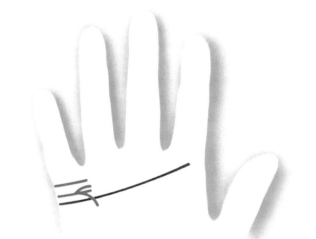

Above. When a third party interferes in, or breaks up a marriage or close love affair, the Line of Affection splits and becomes a three-pronged fork. The middle branch will be the other love.

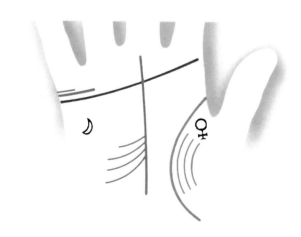

Above. The Mount of Venus ♀ is linked to affairs of the heart. Many small lines running alongside and inside the Line of Life mean that the opposite sex may be difficult to resist.

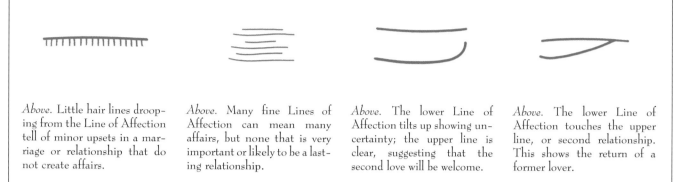

Above. Little hair lines drooping from the Line of Affection tell of minor upsets in a marriage or relationship that do not create affairs.

Above. Many fine Lines of Affection can mean many affairs, but none that is very important or likely to be a lasting relationship.

Above. The lower Line of Affection tilts up showing uncertainty; the upper line is clear, suggesting that the second love will be welcome.

Above. The lower Line of Affection touches the upper line, or second relationship. This shows the return of a former lover.

main Line of Affection (see bottom right, page 88). If it is the woman who has the secret lover, she will have this line. Even if her partner is oblivious to what is going on, he, too, will develop the finer line, which will tell him of the infidelity.

A Line of Affection with a two-pronged fork suggests that, although two people are together, they are 'going their own ways'. The quality of communication may not be very good, to say the least, but for some reason, which may be linked to children or financial issues, the couple may not split up altogether. If the lower branch descends towards the Line of Heart, then separation or divorce is highly likely. A three-pronged fork (see middle right, page 88) is found when a third party interferes in a relationship.

If the Line of Affection has a tiny cross close to the end, but not actually on the line, it can mean that the owner's loved one is not always totally honest, but not necessarily unfaithful.

Many people 'fall in love' with a fantasy. A reasonably happily married woman, for example, might find herself attracted to another man, perhaps at work, because her relationship has become rather predictable. Suddenly she might find that she makes a special effort to look attractive at work. Her whole demeanour begins to change: she becomes livelier, and looks better, perhaps even younger. She starts to think more and more about the man who attracts her so much, and begins to fantasize, often totally unrealistically, about him. In her imagination he becomes another person: glamorous, desirable, interesting, scintillating. In fact, he may be ordinary, plain or even boring. But because she lacks excitement in her life, and is of a romantic, imaginative disposition, she has projected an unrealistic image onto him.

Such projections occur very often, but rarely culminate in an actual affair. The tendency to conjure up a romantic fantasy can happen to anybody, but as women tend to be more romantic than men, they are more likely to succumb to such dreams, which are generally harmless. If the imaginary lover gets seriously out of perspective and looms too large in the world of reality, however, problems inevitably arise. The object of desire may not have any idea that he is worshipped, and if the one who is so enamoured reveals her feelings, it can be terribly embarrassing for the recipient.

When a 'hidden love' takes hold of a person, it can manifest on the hand as a Line of Affection below the Finger of Mercury ☿, but will often be a small line right on the edge of the palm. It will not show clearly, but will be tucked away hidden from view when the palm is examined.

The Line of Fate, which reflects all life's main events, can show people, including lovers, who come into and influence our lives. Lines of Influence rising from the Mount of the Moon ☽ to merge with the Line of Fate (see bottom right, page 88) can each represent a person. These lines are always best when they do not cross or cut into the Line of Fate as this brings some sort of difficulty. Touching the Line of Fate, they bring love affairs and romantic encounters.

Line of Affection		Line of Heart	
Line of Fate		Line of Life	
Line of Head		Line of the Sun	

A LAW UNTO THEMSELVES

The Lines of Head and Heart are usually separate, but sometimes you will see a palm that appears to have a Line of Head but no Line of Heart, or vice versa. In either case, what you are looking at is a combination of the two, called the Simian Line.

The Simian Line is likely to be found on the palms of people who have a strong tendency to be 'a law unto themselves'. The word simian means monkey-like, but do not assume that the owner of such a line will bear any behavioural resemblance to a monkey (the reason why it is so-called will soon be explained). This line involves emotional and other responses, hence its relevance in this chapter. People with this line can find some aspects of relating to others problematic. They may need to understand how this line manifests in their lives and how best to handle the energies created by it.

The Line of Head, in essence, corresponds with mental ability: the way we think and the quality of the mind. The Line of Heart is an indicator of emotional and sexual responses and, to some extent, our capacity for love. When separate, the Lines of Head and Heart allow objectivity and reason to rationalize and temper emotional responses. When the Simian Line is found, it can disrupt this delicate balance because thoughts and feelings are combined.

It is quite rare to find a pure Simian Line on both palms; owners of such will be very subjective and wilful. They will not easily adhere to the usual norms of society, but will be a law unto themselves. In extreme cases, they will be completely ruled by passions and instincts and the law of the jungle will apply, hence the name given to the line. The texture of the palm is very important here: if the skin is hard, a tendency to resist any rules of society will be amplified and the personality may be very self-centred. If the hands and fingers are inflexible, a tendency to refuse to see anything beyond a limited point of view will be further compounded.

This type often feels lot of tension and internal pressure as everything is experienced in an acute way; this can give way to unreasonable outbursts, which can be aggressive. A violent tendency is found when other features, as well as the Simian Line, are present. If the thumb is straight with no waist, a lack of reason will be very marked. When the Simian Line is found on both palms, look out for a short thumb. If it is very bulbous at the top and does not bend back easily under pressure, a violent temper is likely. It may be a good idea to avoid aggravating the owner of such a palm.

If the hands, apart from having Simian Lines, are otherwise normal – and especially if they are flexible – negative traits will be less defined. There can often be a great deal of highly creative energy simmering under the surface, which, if given the

Left. The Simian Line – a combination of the Lines of Heart and Head – is often mistakenly viewed with some trepidation.

opportunity in terms of education and environment, can manifest itself in a powerful, highly individual way.

For a pure simian type — someone with a very defined Simian Line on both hands — all areas of life are experienced with enormous intensity. Powers of concentration can be tremendous as everything on a mental level is also felt emotionally and all feelings simultaneously register mentally. Whatever is chosen in terms of work is therefore crucial, as it will be far better to apply concentrated energies to demanding tasks rather than to other people. Emotions can be so caught up in thought that responses can be, or seem to be, cold and unfeeling. Often, there is little comfort to be found in relationships as the element of sharing can be in short supply. The deep sensitivity of many simian types registers so subjectively that experiencing closeness and harmony in a relationship can be very difficult.

If this line is to be found on the left hand only, it can tell of a rather sheltered early life, or one where the child felt alienated, lonely and misunderstood and apart from the rest of the family. There will be a tendency either to shun responsibility, especially in early life, or at least to defy the rules, be wayward and deliberately awkward. In matters of the heart, there can be a relentless attitude, which demands things to be ideal. The subjective nature can make relationships difficult, as it will be hard to make allowances for the other person and to realize that any harm is being done. Normal Lines of Head and Heart on the right hand improve the ability to realize harmonious relationships, but there will always be a basically intense nature, which can require much love and understanding from a partner.

If the Simian Line is found on the right hand only, physical desires can get out of control. Again, the subjective nature and basic tendency not to see reason can create problems. When such powerful, concentrated energies are applied to a relationship, love can sometimes find expression only through obsession, as there can be some difficulty in articulating the magnitude of innermost feelings. The need to show such intense emotion may be directed mainly through sexual channels; the owner of such a palm would need a partner who also has a strong sex drive, otherwise the needs of the right-handed simian lover could feel excessively demanding.

If you have a Simian Line on one or both palms and have read some books on palmistry, especially those that were written a long time ago, you may have felt a bit concerned about some of the things that have been said about this line. Certainly it can create some problems in terms of the intensification of all your experiences, especially emotional ones and it can sometimes be difficult for others to understand you. Take heart, however, in the knowledge that it is probably better to feel so deeply than not to feel much at all; that your inner depth of subjective and often passionate feeling can be a fount of great creativity; and that your powers of concentration can serve you well, depending on how you choose to use them.

Line of Affection	Line of Heart
Line of Fate	Line of Life
Line of Head	Line of the Sun

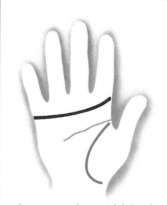

Above. A very long and defined Line of Heart and a rather weak Line of Head. To the untrained eye, such a Line of Heart could be mistaken for a Simian Line.

Above. When the Simian Line is found in the usual position of the Line of Heart, the emphasis will be on emotional intensity and subjectivity. Reason will take second place.

Above. A Simian Line in the usual position of the Line of Head reveals that the thinking processes are intensified and can deepen the powers of concentration.

THE BROKEN HEART

Below. Crisis can affect the health, so when the heart feels as if it is broken, this will also show on the Line of Life, which reflects our well-being. The island on this Line of Life shows the trauma of loss.

Most of us, during the course of our lives, experience some heartache over a lost love. Some of us have more severe loss or disappointment in love to bear and come to terms with. Lost causes, or terrible disappointments that are not linked to personal relationships, can also be heart-breaking, as can emotional deprivation experienced in early life. The heart is the seat of all our emotions and so is naturally affected by all that we feel. Happiness as well as sorrow registers there and, in turn, is mirrored on the palm.

Remember to examine both hands so that you will be able to tell if an emotional crisis has already happened, or if it is still to come. Be gentle in explaining your findings to the person whose hands you are looking at: if there is going to be some unavoidable pain, be diplomatic and thoughtful to avoid causing anxiety.

A long Line of Heart literally indicates a great capacity to give and receive love, whilst a shorter line will tell of a cooler and less emotional response in matters of love and to others generally. A short line will be one that starts at the edge of the palm and ends under the Finger of Saturn ♄. It is rare to find an even-shorter line that terminates under the Finger of the Sun ☉. Such a Line of Heart would belong to a very cold and unloving person.

Severe heart-break can actually manifest on the hand as a broken Line of Heart (see above left). This is quite rare and, when found, there is likely to be a 'sister' line or lines, or a square, that will help to heal the heart and repair and heal the break. Other factors on the hand will reveal how well a person is likely to recover from acute loss or trauma. A broken Line of Heart sometimes corresponds with a shock to the heart itself and can affect its function. Without the help of sister lines or a square, a broken Line of Heart can mean that the loss and heart-break may never really be healed and no one else shall take the place of the lost loved one.

The Line of Fate reveals our aims, purpose and direction, so if a great loss has occurred, it will also show on this line. When the Line of Fate fragments, there will be a time of having to reorientate and redefine a future after a familiar pattern of existence with a loved one has gone. The shock of a great loss will register on the hand of a person who has had a long-standing and happy relationship, but if the quality of a life shared with another has been very harmonious, the actual length of time spent together will not be so relevant; the sensitivity and devotion of the bereaved or abandoned one will also contribute to the magnitude of the feeling of loss.

Above. The terrible mental depression which follows a profound loss is often shown by a Line of Affection dipping down to the Line of Head, creating an indentation.

When a separation from a partner happens through death or otherwise and is a source of profound sadness, the Line of Affection can dip down to the Line of Head; and where the two lines meet, it will create a defined spot or small indentation, indicating the accompanying mental shock (see page 92, bottom).

Small hair lines, drooping from the Line of Heart, rather like a sad little fringe, mean a series of small disappointments in love. They can also show flirtatiousness, each line representing a different lover. If the Line of Heart is thus marked on a long portion of the line, it may mean that there is some psychological quirk or fear that unconsciously prevents a relationship with someone who would not turn out to be a disappointment.

For someone with stiff, inflexible fingers and thumbs, a great change in life in terms of losing a loved one could be more difficult as the ability to adapt will not come easily. Such people tend to have rather rigid routines; if they are changed, it could further compound the trauma of loss and heart-break, as all the usual patterns of existence with a partner will be no more.

The Girdle of Venus is like a secondary Line of Heart (see The Artistic Hand, pages 50-51 and The Passionate Lover, pages 80-81). It begins between the Fingers of Jupiter ♃ and Saturn ♄ and ends between the Fingers of the Sun ☉ and Mercury ☿. When found in the palm it can promote a volatile disposition and can also add spark and zest to creative pursuits. If, however, the Girdle of Venus touches a Line of Affection beneath the Finger of Mercury, it can create problems. Moodiness can sometimes erupt, frustration and anger can be difficult to control with emotions swelling like a tidal wave of wrath. Such feelings can be destructive to a relationship. When the Girdle of Venus is actually caught up in a Line of Affection, it will be the partner that suffers the brunt of overheated emotions. These may have nothing to do with the relationship, but stem from other areas of unhappiness or discontent. We often hurt most the ones we love.

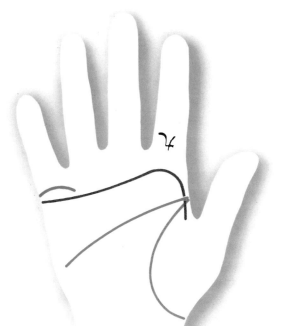

Above. A Line of Heart that suddenly changes course as it reaches the Mount of Jupiter ♃ to curve downwards cutting through the beginning of the Lines of Head and Life can mean that there is some inability to see others for what they are. Not only can this lack of clarity affect romance, it can also create problems in the choice of friends. The main difficulty here can be misplaced love or friendship, which is often not fully returned, or is truly unrequited.

Below. The Line of Heart shown here extends right across the palm, not stopping on it, but curving round the edge of the Mount of Jupiter ♃. This can denote enormous idolatry which will inevitably end in hurt feelings because the object of such worship is a mere mortal. This line also brings a tendency to deny disappointment, so if the partner is not worthy of such love it will not be acknowledged, and heartache will tend to register deeply inside.

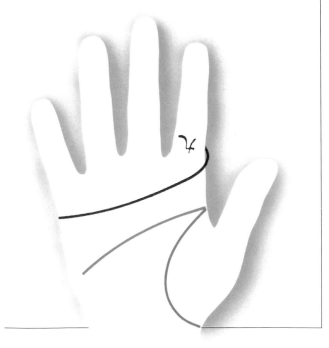

——— Line of Affection	——— Line of Heart
——— Line of Fate	——— Line of Life
——— Line of Head	——— Line of the Sun

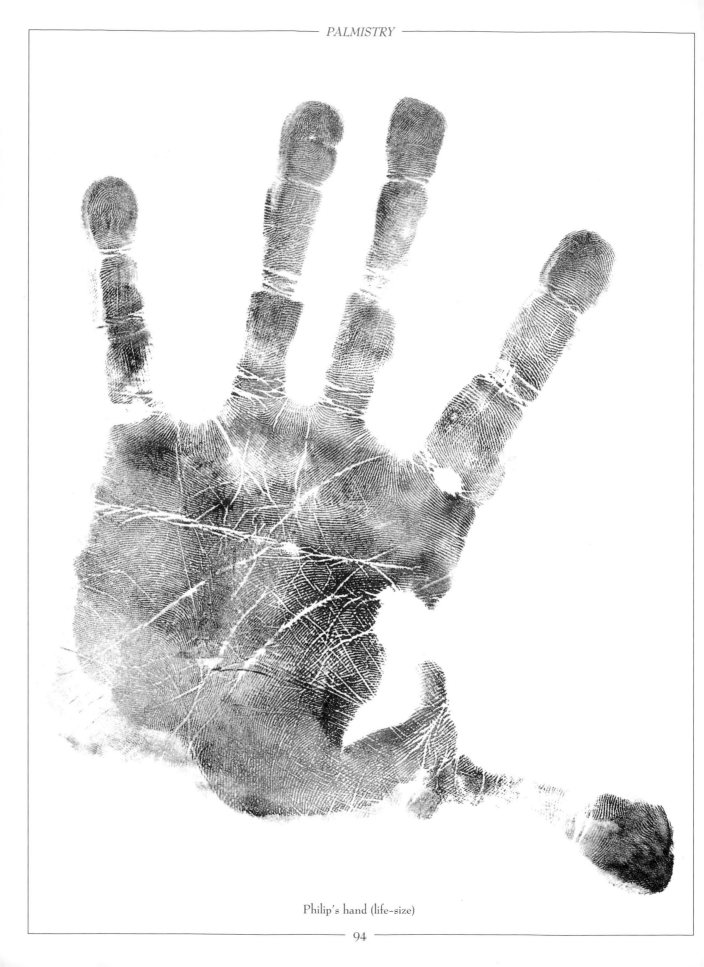

Philip's hand (life-size)

SAMPLE READING
PHILIP'S HAND

This is the left palm of a right-handed man in his early forties. Many factors on this palm denote a rather unusual character, who is intense, loving, sensual and practical at the same time. The large, square palm reveals his pragmatic side. Large hands like Philip's are often very good at intricate tasks. He is a computer consultant whose work requires attention to fine detail, analysis, and the ability to create new ways of doing things.

There are two unusual features on this hand. Philip has a Simian Line, a combination of the Lines of Head and Heart. The second rather unusual factor is the thumb. Note how flexible it is, standing away from the palm, almost at a right angle to it.

A Simian Line, as you have learned, can create intensity and sometimes aggression. The angle of the thumb reveals much about will-power and reasoning ability: the more rigid the thumb, the more stubborness and resistance to other people's ideas there will be. Philip's very flexible thumb indicates humanitarian attitudes and dislike of overt aggression. His inner tension will therefore rarely manifest itself belligerently towards others. As the Simian Line appears only on his left hand, Philip will have a basic tendency to experience life on an intense level. His energies are condensed, in that the thinking and feeling sides of him combine to create determination and a terrific ability to concentrate. His Simian Line is found in the usual position of the Line of Heart, which reveals that the feeling side of Philip predominates. Such a line set lower on the hand would mean that the intellect rules the feelings.

Philip has a very wide and well-developed Mount of Venus on both palms. As this mount corresponds with love and warmth, it shows that Philip has a powerful capacity for love, and that he is lusty and sensual. A Simian Line found on the left hand often contributes to fundamental sensuality. Together with a full Mount of Venus, love, desires and passions are even more amplified. But Philip is not ruled by his desires. Although he appreciates women a great deal and is something of a flirt, he has a loyal disposition and has never been unfaithful. Flirtatiousness is indicated on this palm by the little feathery lines on the Simian Line, which is ruled by the Line of Heart, rather than the Line of Head.

If the Simian Line and such a pronounced Mount of Venus were found on the right hand instead of the left, then the combination would have a very different meaning. Sensuality and passion could be difficult to cope with. If the Simian Line and large Mount of Venus were found on both palms, then life would be ruled by unbridled passions, probably with dire consequences. Found only on the left palm, as in Philip's case, these features are a much better sign. The fundamental impassioned, sensual disposition is tempered by reason, bringing the ability to enjoy life and love to the full and to realize more depth and intensity of experience than many people do.

Philip, in summary, uses his impassioned nature well in his life. His ability to apply himself to his work in a dedicated fashion is as equally strong as his capacity to be loving. He is an 'all-or-nothing' person, who will not do anything in a half-hearted way.

COMMON QUESTIONS

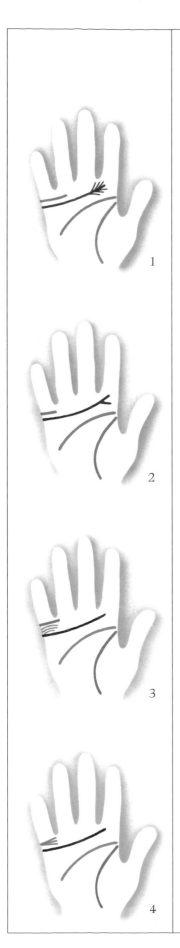

1. Will I be happy in love?
   Yes, according to your palm. The lines splaying out at the end of your Line of Heart can mean great happiness. Enjoy it.

2. Although I love my partner deeply, I often feel the need to be and express myself. This worries me. Why do I feel this way?
   Your long, forked Line of Heart shows your loving nature. The wide gap between your Lines of Head and Life shows your need for spontaneous self-expression, while maintaining love and loyalty.

3. I have had a lot of disappointing, unsettling affairs, which have made me feel empty and miserable. Will this change?
   Yes, eventually. When the time is right, a constant love will be realized. A strong, clear Line of Affection above the ones that droop, shows you can look forward to a durable relationship.

4. I am married, but fantasize about having an affair and so does my husband. Should we make our dreams become reality?
   Your Line of Affection splits into a trident fork indicating a third party. Affairs may not make either of you happy. Be extremely careful.

5. We are in love. Will it grow?
   A Line of Influence makes its way to the marriage sector situated below the Finger of Mercury ☿. Love will indeed further blossom.

6. Will the relationship that I am in at the moment enhance my life generally?
   Probably not, as a Line of Influence cuts through rather than blending in with your Line of Fate. There could be trouble ahead.

7. Why do I get so upset with my lover if she even looks at another man?
   Your very long Line of Heart can be a bit obsessive. Your Line of Affection is strong. Jealousy can be destructive. Try to temper your feelings.

8. I am so often misunderstood, and I am often angry and upset wth my partner. Why is this?
   Your Simian Line shows great intensity which is best applied to challenges and not people.

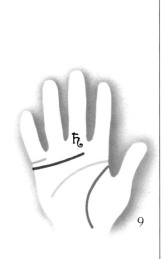

9

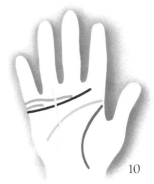

10

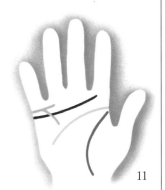

11

12

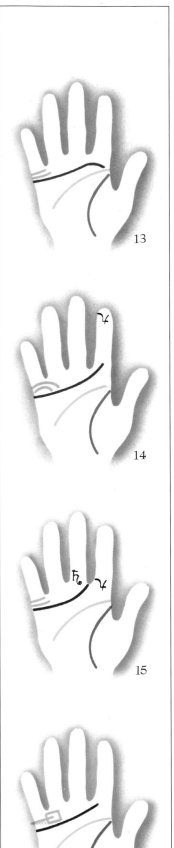

13

14

15

16

9. My girlfriend has accused me of being a bit cold. Does my hand say I am?
Your Line of Heart ends under Saturn ♄. Your girl-friend's is probably longer. You may not be very romantic but you are loyal and dependable.

10. I am female, married and a famous public figure. I am fascinated by a beautiful younger man. What should I do about it?
A line from the marriage area cuts through your Line of the Sun. Beware of slander and loss.

11. Our marriage is dreadful. We fight all the time. What will happen?
The lower fork of your Line of Affection cuts through your Line of Heart. This means that divorce or separation is very likely.

12. I feel I will only ever love the one I am with. We have been together for four years. Am I being realistic?
You have one clear, strong and lasting Line of Affection. Count your blessings and enjoy your rare love.

13. I am unsure about my sexual orientation. Does this show on my hand?
Your Line of Heart dips towards the start of your Line of Head, which sometimes means same-sex love or bisexuality, especially if found on both palms. Accept yourself and be happy.

14. My lover is perfect. I adore her. But she upsets me by being critical and even contemptuous towards me. Why is this?
Your Line of Heart curves up to Jupiter ♃, showing your idealism. No one is perfect. A good relationship needs mutual respect.

15. My boyfriend wants us to abandon everything to live in the country and make wood carvings for a living. I do not want to. What should we do?
Your Line of Heart ends between the Mounts of Jupiter ♃ and Saturn ♄ showing that you are practical and realistic. Your boyfriend may be more of a dreamer. Do what is best for both of you. Perhaps you could compromise.

16. We have had a lot of difficulties throughout our marriage but want to stay together and make a go of our relationship. Is this wise?
Your Line of Affection shows little lines drooping from it, indicating problems, but the protective square will help you to sort things out satisfactorily.

Line of Affection		Line of Heart	
Line of Fate		Line of Life	
Line of Head		Line of the Sun	

Chapter Five

HEALTH MATTERS

We often take good health for granted until we get ill. A good diet, together with enough exercise and rest are all essential for a healthy body, but our attitude is vital: illness and disease often spring from being out of sorts either emotionally or mentally, or frequently both.

Emotional or mental illness reflects the stress we encounter in our busy, and in many ways unnatural, existences. We are all under a great deal of pressure. No wonder so many of us get frayed around the edges or split at the seams.

The tone, colour, texture and resilience of our palms, together with certain marks and lines, can reveal a great deal about our physical condition. The finger-nails are also a good barometer of health. Palmistry can help us to identify vulnerable areas or those under stress. This chapter shows where they may be found. The palms represent every aspect of our being – body, mind and spirit – all of which must be in equilibrium in order for us to maintain a healthy life.

THE HEALTHY HAND

We only really appreciate our health when we have known how it feels to be ill. The palm can reveal a great deal about health, but when carrying out a reading, it is generally the area that requires the most tact. Be very careful not to jump to conclusions or worry someone unnecessarily. If there are indications of ill health, then explain this gently. If the person is feeling below par or has symptoms of illness, suggest that professional help is sought. Remember that it is not what you say but the way that you say it that matters. We all experience illness from time to time, but tend to forget that the body has amazing powers of self-healing and recovery.

Some people ignore illness till it becomes serious; others rush off to the doctor with the slightest symptom of ill health. Doctors often prescribe placebos and the patient gets better because his or her need for attention has been satisfied. This suggests the illness was all in the mind in the first place.

When you are looking at hands to find out about health, firstly feel the overall 'bounce' or resilience of the palm. Press it lightly with your fingertips. If it is healthy, it should feel fairly firm and bounce slightly when you release the pressure.

The centre of the palm is known as the Plain of Mars ♂. It is especially important in relation to health and should have a firm feel to it. Two other relevant areas on the palm are the Mounts of Mars. One is located just inside the beginning of the Line of Life and tells much about energy. It should not be too flat and crinkled, unless the owner of the hand is quite old, and should be firm to the touch; neither should it be too highly developed or very red, as these signs tell of a rather aggressive temper on a short fuse. The other Mount of Mars is found on the outer edge of the palm and, again, there should be a firm feeling to it. When the Mars areas are resilient it helps the entire body to generate energy and to be resistant to illness.

The colour of the hand, too, is important. It should not be too pale as this suggests a lack of energy or enthusiasm, or both, and sometimes means there will be a rather cool emotional response to life. The opposite applies to very red hands, especially when they have a swollen, pumped-up look to them, which suggests blood pressure may be high.

If we are tired we are more prone to illness. Small horizontal lines on the top phalanges (see middle left) suggest that the subject is tired and may need a few early nights to restore the body's energies. If, however, the person tells you that he or she *has* been having enough rest, energy reserves are depleted for some reason. Suggest that more rest, or even a holiday, might be a good idea, as people can get weary, not just from over-exertion, but from tedium as well. Boredom can dilute the body's energies so a change could indeed be as good as a rest.

The colour of the lines on the palm should also be taken into account. If they have a yellow tinge, or brownish look, there may be a problem linked to the condition of the blood, such as anaemia, or a slight malfunction of the liver. Very pale lines can have the same meaning. If the lines are very red, it can be linked to some fieriness in the personality. The palms should not be

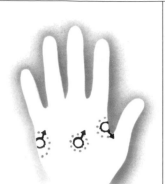

Above. The Plain of Mars ♂, found in the centre of the palm, and the two Mounts of Mars on either side. If they are resilient when touched, but not too developed, they reveal a fairly hardy constitution.

Above. Horizontal lines on the top phalanges of the fingers indicate tiredness. If you have these lines, think about taking a break, getting more sleep or perhaps changing your life in some way.

Above. The colour of the lines is very revealing about health. The Line of Life shown here becomes progressively redder as it swoops down towards its end at the wrist. This can mean that the body is rather acidic.

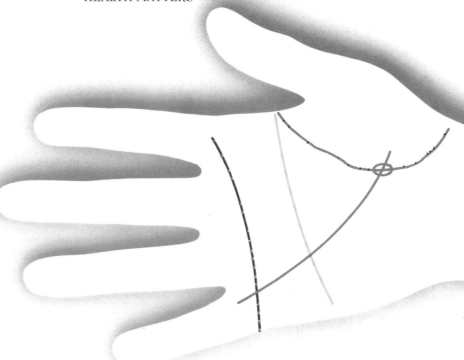

Right. The Line of Mercury is found slanting from the area below the Line of Heart towards the lower part of the Line of Life. Not everybody has this line. When it is absent, this bodes well for health in an overall way. Its presence, however, does not have an ominous meaning, but can suggest that the nervous system is rather sensitive. This line is also known as the 'Liver Line' and is linked, in various ways, to the digestive processes. People with this line should keep to a sensible diet and avoid excesses. It is always a better sign when the Line of Mercury does not actually touch the Line of Life, as this can undermine the health. This line is examined further on pages 106-107.

very damp, as this can reveal nervousness.

There are various special marks that, when found on certain lines, have something to say about health. Crosses on the Line of Life can mean a period of ill health; dots on any line can indicate the same; and a chained look to any line can signify weakness. A chain on the Line of Head, for example, signifies mental weakness. Remember to examine both hands: what shows on the left hand has occured already, or is an influence that is currently phasing out; and what is found on the right hand is yet to come (the opposite applies to a left-handed person).

The texture of the palm can be revealing. If the skin is hard, but the hands do not do manual work and are not exposed to harsh chemicals, it can mean that there is a lot of inner pressure that can have an adverse effect on the health and sometimes the arteries in particular. If the hands are very soft and flexible, almost as though they have no solid bones inside them, and are also rather pale, there can be some problem linked to blood pressure. There may be little energy and a visit to a doctor would be advisable.

The finger-nails can also reveal health problems. The nails take about nine months to grow out from the finger and a defect on the nail can show how long ago a problem began, or was experienced. The illustrations (see below) show typical health indications on the finger-nails.

——— Line of Affection	——— Line of Heart
——— Line of Fate	——— Line of Life
——— Line of Head	Line of the Sun

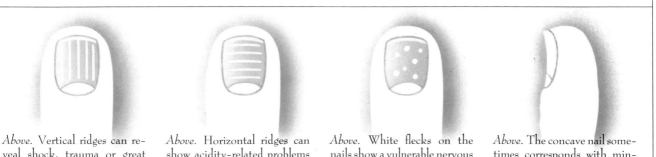

Above. Vertical ridges can reveal shock, trauma or great demands that have been made on physical resources.

Above. Horizontal ridges can show acidity-related problems and are mostly found on the hands of older people.

Above. White flecks on the nails show a vulnerable nervous system, whilst spots indicate a weak constitution.

Above. The concave nail sometimes corresponds with mineral deficiency. It can also reveal physical tension.

YOU ARE WHAT YOU EAT

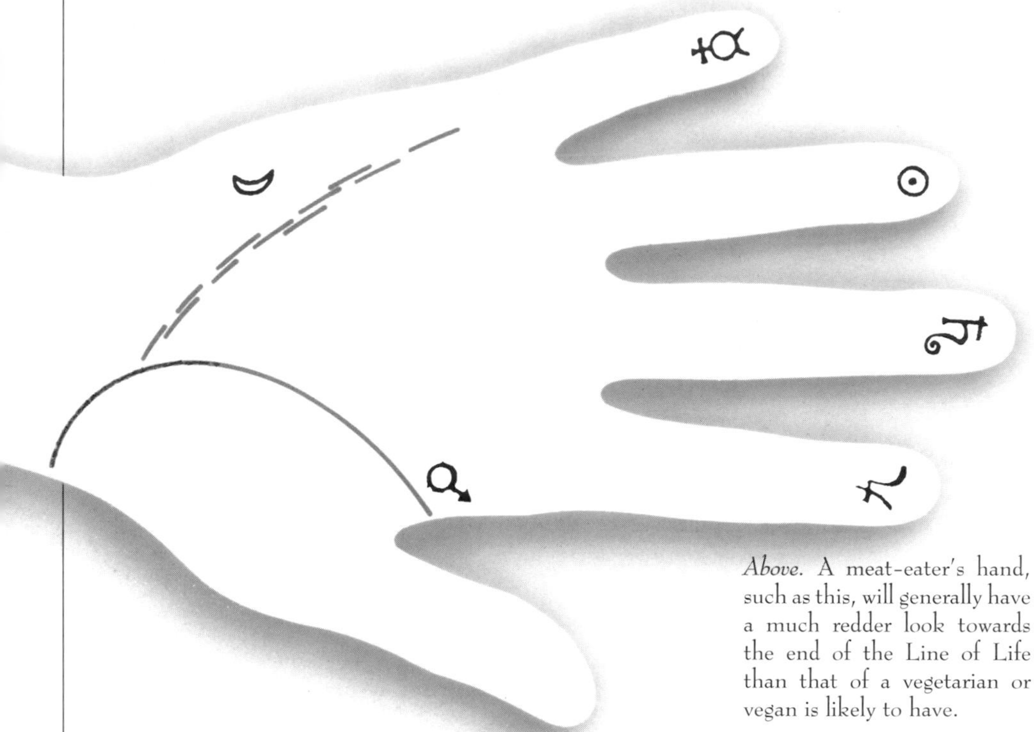

Above. A meat-eater's hand, such as this, will generally have a much redder look towards the end of the Line of Life than that of a vegetarian or vegan is likely to have.

Above. A branch from the Line of Life towards Mercury ☿ is known as the Line of Mercury. When this is wavy, it can show a tendency to disorders of the gastro-enteric tract, which could also be stress-related.

Above. When the lower phalanges of the fingers are very full and fleshy, they are likely to belong to a gourmet. Sometimes this can lead to gluttony, especially when the whole hand is 'puffed up'.

Above. The Mount of the Moon ☽ is divided into three sections, each corresponding with a different area of the body. Marks here can indicate vulnerabilities to diet.

Our primary instinct is to survive, which means that we must eat. Most of us eat far more than we really need or is good for us. Food creates energy, but the digestion of it also requires energy: when we overeat, we can, in effect, be taxing our body unnecessarily by creating a lot of hard work for our digestive system. When someone goes on a special diet for health reasons, he or she will often look and feel better and have far more energy and enthusiasm.

These days, people are paying more attention to their diet than ever before. There are many reasons for this, the first being choice. In the past, people had to eat what was readily available unless they were rich enough to do otherwise. Secondly, travel and communications today allow us to experiment with and enjoy food from virtually anywhere in the world.

The mounts and the fingers correspond with various areas of the body. If the lower phalange of the Finger of Jupiter ♃ has a flabby, soft feel to it, it can indicate a tendency to indigestion, so acidic foods should be avoided. If it is thin and 'waisted' compared to the other fingers, nervousness or throat troubles may occur.

A grille, or crossbars on the Mount of Saturn ♄ can show a tendency to suffer from varicose veins or haemorrhoids. Vitamin E can be of benefit in such instances. These marks can also indicate depression and pessimism. Found on the Mount of the Sun ☉, these marks, or an island, can be linked to the heart, so a sensible diet and life-style including enough exercise is advisable. Islands, grilles and crossed lines on the Mount of Mercury ☿ often accompany a tendency to nervous conditions, which may give rise to dyspepsia, liverishness or other stomach troubles. The B vitamins can be a great help here. If the Mount of Mars ♂ is red, or has a grille, island or crossbars on it, it can reveal a quick temper and a predisposition to inflammatory physical conditions.

If there is a grille, island or star on the Mount of the Moon ☽, it can reveal health problems. The location of these marks reveals where in the body the problems are likely to be found. On the top area of the mount, these marks show a tendency to inflammation of the bowels or other intestinal disorders, which can be reduced by making sure the diet has plenty of fibre. Marks on the middle part of the mount can indicate tendencies to rheumatism or gout, so rich food and drink should be consumed in moderation. The lower area is linked to the bladder and kidneys; if it is marked by the above and has a mottled look to it as well, it will be important to drink plenty of water to keep the system well flushed out.

The colour of the palm is very revealing when it comes to health matters. When the palm is very pale and the lines upon it also lack colour, it can mean that the diet is deficient in iron. In such instances, the palm is usually soft to the touch as well. When doing a reading for someone with such a palm, try to establish whether or not there are any further symptoms of iron-deficiency. Is there a tendency to tire easily or to be very sensitive to stuffy, airless environments, for example?

A series of chains between the Lines of Head and Life can often be found when the head is, literally, congested. Sinusitis is a common disorder, but is usually found in those whose bodies react negatively to dairy products. Catarrh is revealed on the palm in the same way, and can also be a result of milk allergy. Fat-free milk or vegetarian cheeses often benefit the sinus sufferer.

Sinusitis can create headaches, lethargy and depression. When it does, there will be tiny lines drooping from the Line of Head, and sometimes a blurred look at the end of the Line of Head (see Depression and Anxiety, pages 110-111).

Remember never to draw strident conclusions about someone's health from the palm. If there is an indication of a diet that is deficient in some way, be careful to establish the cause through careful questioning. And never recommend any major dietary changes. Always insist that someone consults a dietician if you think there may be a serious deficiency.

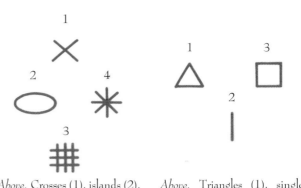

Above. Crosses (1), islands (2), grilles (3) and sometimes stars (4) on the mounts can indicate illness linked to diet deficiencies or over-indulgence.

Above. Triangles (1), single vertical lines (2) and squares (3) show good health. When found on a mount, they reveal a healthy diet.

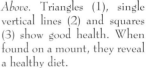

	Line of Affection		Line of Heart
	Line of Fate		Line of Life
	Line of Head		Line of the Sun

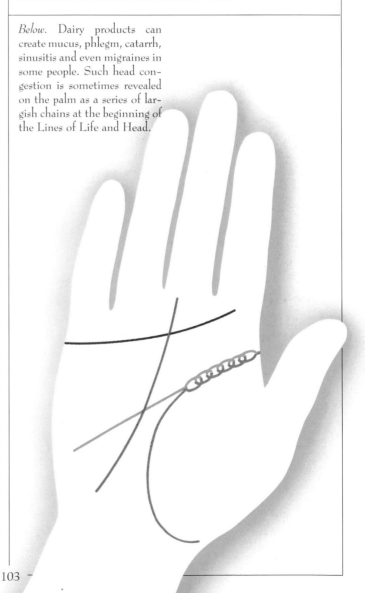

Below. Dairy products can create mucus, phlegm, catarrh, sinusitis and even migraines in some people. Such head congestion is sometimes revealed on the palm as a series of largish chains at the beginning of the Lines of Life and Head.

Heart and back problems

Heart and back problems are extremely common and often very serious. Certain lines and features of the palm can reveal a lot about current and potential problems in these two areas.

A healthy heart

The heart is the centre of our entire being. All our feelings register on the Line of Heart and, to a lesser extent, on some other lines and features of the palm. The healthy action, or any malfunction, of the heart, can also be reflected on the Line of Heart.

The finger-nails, too, can reveal a lot about the health of our most vital organ. The moon at the base of the nail is of particular relevance. When you are looking at the nails, remember that some people do not push down their cuticles, so their moons may be covered. The moons should be showing, but should not, ideally, be too large, as this shows a rather over-active heart. If the moons cannot be seen even when the cuticles are clear of the nails, the reverse may apply.

If there is a blue tinge on the curve of the moon, then the circulation may be very poor. This, in turn, may be linked to a heart defect. A brownish colour can mean there is some problem with the liver or the blood. The nails themselves should be pink. If they are very pale, there may be a rather cool disposition and perhaps some anaemia.

Islands and chains on the Line of Heart can mean that the organ is weak. This may cause a lack of energy and impetus. If there is a series of dots on this line, together with a similar marking on the Line of Life, this can mean that the action of the heart is erratic, emotionally or physically.

Do not frighten yourself or anyone else by making rash judgements based on the state of a Line of Heart or the finger-nails. Time takes its toll, so do not expect an older person to have as strong and resilient a heart as a young person. Anyone who feels unaccountably tired, is rendered easily breathless or suffers from a lot of what feels like heartburn should seek medical attention immediately. This little book does not make a doctor of you, but is written to help you to understand how the hand reveals all aspects of your being, including the health.

Back problems

There is an old saying, 'You are only as strong as your back'. Many people suffer from tensions that affect the muscles and bones of the back. The stresses and strains of modern life are often difficult to deal with and can cause or contribute to back problems.

Some people are more predisposed to suffering from backache than others. There are many wonderful ways of strengthening a weak back, such as the Alexander Technique, which can affect the entire being in a positive way, promoting balance, harmony and self-awareness.

When we are feeling despondent or bowed down by the burdens of life, this is often reflected in bad posture. This is not only bad for the back,

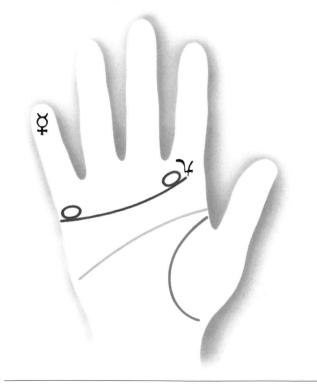

Below. Clear, elongated islands on the Line of Heart have different meanings depending on their location. Close to the Finger of Mercury ☿, an island can reveal a minor heart problem that is likely to have been noticed and treated in early life. Close to the Mount of Jupiter ♃, an island can indicate an early emotional trauma.

Left. The finger-nails can reveal much about the strength of the back. If the nails are narrow and arched as shown here, the back may be weak and prone to problems.

	Line of Affection
	Line of Fate
	Line of Head
	Line of Heart
	Line of Life
	Line of the Sun

but can also adversely affect the internal organs, which cannot function well if they are compressed within a wilting framework. Many disorders of the digestive system, chest and even heart can be aggravated, or even created, by a distorted posture.

The back can effectively 'give' under pressure. This often occurs during a crucial period when a person feels overwhelmed by anxiety and unable to cope. When life is extremely difficult, and the energy to respond to it is at a low ebb, the palm can develop many tiny lines running all over its surface, which will fade out as the body's energies are restored.

Back problems can also be brought about by emotional pressure. When a person feels severely thwarted and unable to exert the necessary will-power to deal with a crisis, the back may respond by making movement difficult, even impossible in severe cases. This can be an unconscious way of avoiding difficulties: if one feels paralysed by pain, it is impossible to take action to improve a galling, frustrating or perhaps threatening situation. Past emotional trauma can register in the back to create possible problems in the future. Crises will be revealed on the Lines of the left hand (see Pressure and Trauma, pages 112-113).

The finger-nails are good indicators of the strength and health of the back. When they are narrow and arched, there is likely to be a weakness somewhere in the back. If one finger-nail has a higher arch than the others, it will sometimes correspond with an area of the spine. Found on the nail of the Finger of Jupiter ♃, the upper back may hold a lot of tension that will subsequently affect the lower areas. The Finger of Saturn ♄, if arched, can indicate mid-back problems. The nail of the Finger of the Sun ☉ can be linked to the lumbar area, and the Finger of Mercury ☿ can correspond with the lower vertebrae. Do not confuse the arched nail with the claw-like one, which is explained on page 19.

Above. A star on the Line of Heart means that the heart itself is under strain. If this appears on a palm, the owner must take more care of his or her health. Sometimes, this mark corresponds with a major shock. Fatigue or any other physical symptoms should not be ignored. A medical check-up would be wise.

Below. Dots on the Line of Heart can indicate emotional stress and anxiety. If the dots are red, or have a red tinge to them, it can mean that unhappy feelings have registered very deeply.

Left. If the moons have a blue tinge, the circulation will be very poor. The heart may not be functioning well and the body is likely to be below par. If the whole nail has this blue tint, it is likely that a heart condition has already been identified and treatment has been given for it.

Left. The 'half moons' on the nails can vary greatly. They should be visible but not too large. Very large moons, such as the one shown here, can sometimes mean that the heart is working hard. There are exceptions, however: large moons are often a sign of caring so can be found on the fingers of people involved in philanthropic professions.

Minor ailments

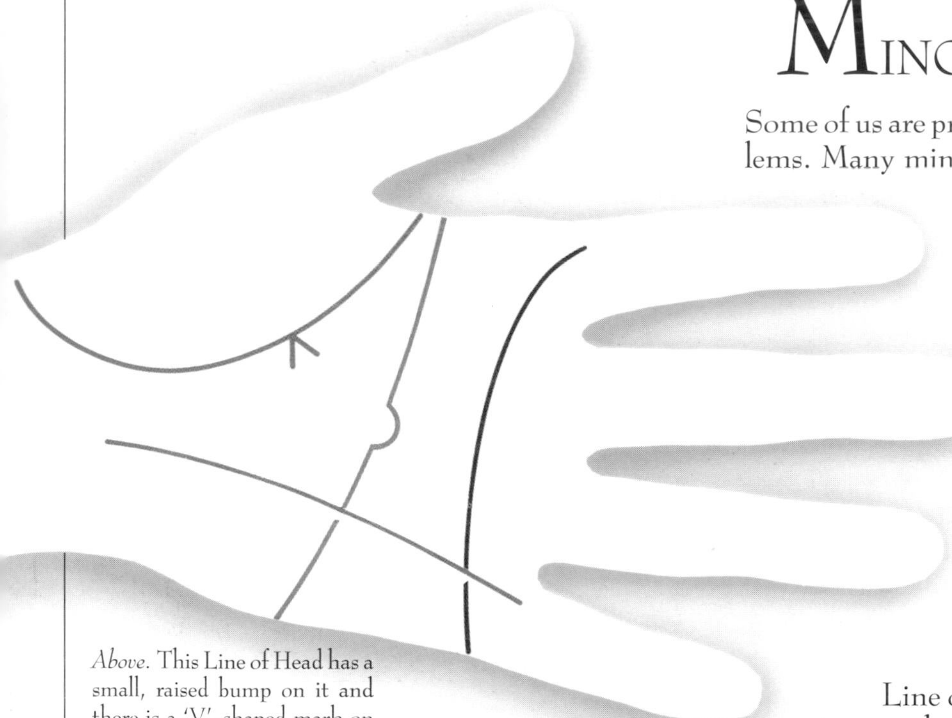

Some of us are predisposed to certain health problems. Many minor ailments can manifest on the hand, and each line is often directly linked with a vulnerable area of the body.

The Line of Head not only reveals a great deal about how one thinks, but can also indicate physical ailments that affect the head, such as eye problems, headaches and migraines in particular (see Pressure and Trauma, pages 112-113).

Poor vision will manifest on the Line of Head in various ways, depending on the severity of the problem. When there is eye strain, you are likely to find a small bump on the Line of Head and an unusual mark on the Line of Life composed of two little lines converging, like an open-ended triangle (see above). If sight has been weak from birth, then you are likely to find a small, rather eye-shaped mark on both Lines of Head. Be careful not to confuse this with an island, which reveals some mental malaise or disability.

Sometimes you may find tiny indentations on one or more of the fingernails, which look like pinpricks. These often correspond with a tendency to suffer from skin complaints such as eczema or psoriasis, but usually on the hands or limbs rather than the body as a whole.

The Line of Mercury (see The Healthy Hand, pages 100-101) is linked to the body and mind in several ways. Of all the lines on the palm, this one can be the most confusing. When looked at in the context of health, it can sometimes be a good sign, sometimes bad, depending on the quality of the line in question.

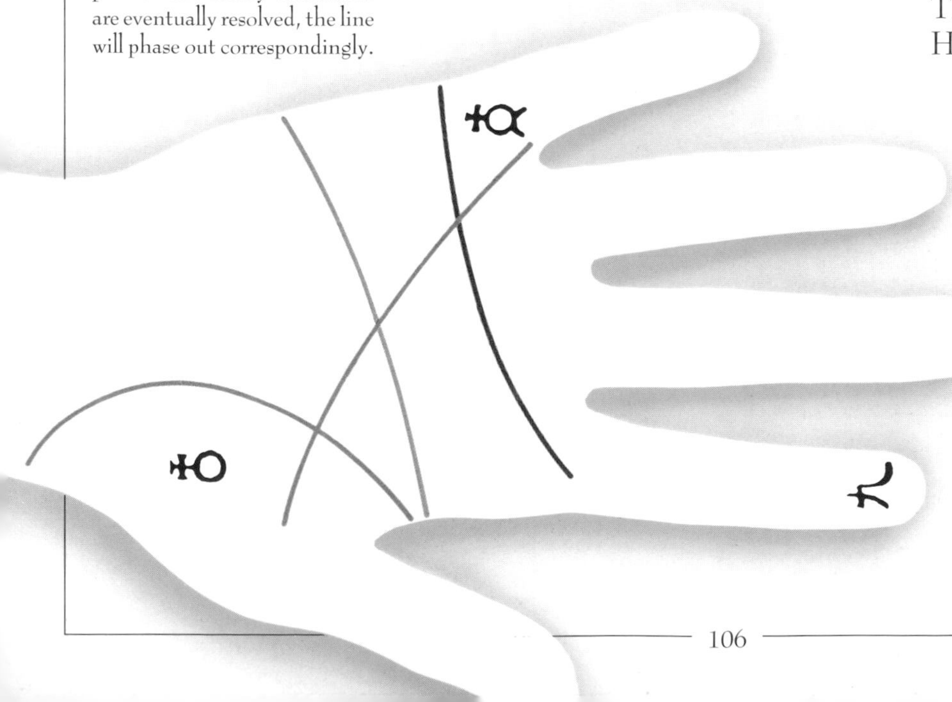

A 'perfect' Line of Mercury (see left) originates at the bottom centre of the palm. It is not split, fragmented or twisted, running a

Above. This Line of Head has a small, raised bump on it and there is a 'V'-shaped mark on the Line of Life. If one or both of these marks are found, then eye strain is likely.

Below. Family influences can sometimes have an adverse effect on one's health. This is shown here by the Line of Mercury, which rises from the Mount of Venus ♀ and cuts through the Line of Life as it courses up the palm towards the Mount of Mercury ☿. As problematic family conditions are eventually resolved, the line will phase out correspondingly.

clear course up to the Mount of Mercury ☿. Such a well-formed line is a rarity. Although it is generally considered better not to have this line at all, when it is perfectly formed it is actually an excellent indication of potential balance between the mind and body. It enhances involvement and interest in all that is undertaken.

People without this line will usually have a strong stomach and nervous system. Resilience to illness will be enhanced. If the line exists, it will not necessarily follow that there will be illness, but there will probably be some delicacy and resistence to illness may sometimes be below par.

When the Line of Mercury begins within the Mount of Venus ♀ and crosses the Line of Life on its way to the Mount of Mercury ☿ (see bottom left) it means that family matters can be difficult to contend with. The feeling of being bound to the family is even more acute when other features are also present: a small, weak thumb, a short Finger of Jupiter ♃ and a soft palm respectively indicate a lack of will-power, confidence and energy. In such cases, illness can sometimes result as a rather sad and desperate means of avoiding family pressures.

Some people need very little sleep and are fine with just a few hours of repose. This is often the case when the Line of Mercury begins with an island (see below), and often there is an ability to 'cat nap' for a few minutes and wake refreshed and invigorated. This island neither signifies insomnia nor affects the health negatively, though some people with this mark may think they need more sleep than they really do.

When someone is not getting enough rest, or the quality of sleep is poor, you are likely to find fine, horizontal lines on the top phalange of the fingers. These little lines are often common on the hands of elderly people, but on the hand of someone young it may simply mean a few early nights will be of benefit and then the lines will disappear. If they do not, and the palm as a whole is not springy and resilient, especially at the centre, then there may be fatigue caused by more than mere tiredness and medical advice should be sought.

Hand shapes can also reveal how likely we are to suffer from minor ailments. People with square, spatulate and elementary hands will tend to be

quite resistant to minor illness in an overall way, as long as the palm does not feel too hard. Conic, philosophic and pointed hands usually belong to people who are less hardy. This is because the more delicate the temperament, the more vulnerable the body will be to minor problems.

Minor illness suffered by spatulate-handed people, who are very often healthy, active types, could be associated with over-activity. Likewise, sickness experienced by square-handed people, especially if the surface of the palm is hard, may often be linked with overwork. Minor health conditions and malaise affecting the pointed or philosophic hand are often highly likely to be linked to nervous over-exertion. Elementary-handed types sometimes harbour an encroaching illness, but can be so habit-bound that they do not notice symptoms until they get serious.

	Line of Affection		Line of Heart
	Line of Fate		Line of Life
	Line of Head		Line of the Sun

Below. There are two islands on this Line of Mercury. The lower island can mean that not much sleep is needed. The island higher up on the line can indicate a fear of illness, even when there are no health problems. This mark can bring hypochondria at worst or an overtly fussy and anxious attitude in matters relating to diet and life-style, which can dilute enjoyment of eating, drinking and making merry.

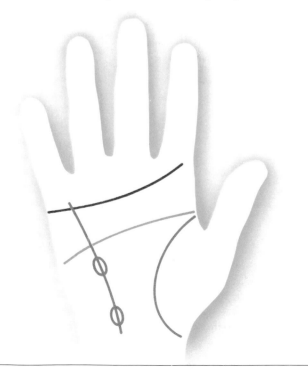

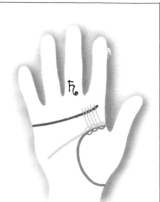

Above. Chains and islands always indicate some sort of problem. Here they are bonding the lines of mind and body in fear and uncertainty, experienced in early life.

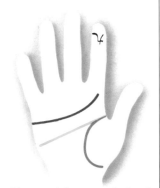

Above. Inhibition, a lack of confidence and a 'faint heart' creating limitation are shown in the tie at the beginning of the Lines of Life and Head. A lack of imagination is shown by the straight Line of Head.

Above. Dreamy, often unrealistic thinking is shown in this very sloping, faint Line of Head. This can be highly creative, especially if the hand as a whole is not too soft. A soft hand means that creativity may not be utilized.

ALL IN THE MIND

If you showed three people the same picture and asked each one to describe it, it is very likely that each person would have a different way of seeing it. We all have a unique way of perceiving life and projecting our ideas, thoughts and feelings into our experiences. We create our own realities through our needs and attitudes. Many illnesses are psychosomatic: the body reflecting emotional or spiritual needs that are somehow not met. A person who enjoys very good health is likely to have naturally, or to have acquired, a harmonious inner state.

A difficult or disturbing childhood can often set the scene for future emotional difficulties that affect the mind and, in turn, the body. The first portion of the Line of Life (the part under the Mount of Jupiter ♃) and other lines interacting with it, can reveal a great deal about early experiences. The Lines of Life and Head are sometimes bonded at the beginning by a series of little chains (see top left). Tiny lines growing out from the chains and rising towards the Mount of Saturn ♄ shows that considerable early difficulty was likely to have affected the health adversely.

Childhood difficulties can manifest in various other ways on the hand. The left hand will reveal what has happened in the past, whilst the right will show how the past influences have, or will, affect the future and the personality. If there is a close tie to the Lines of Life and Head (see middle left), which continues some distance on the lines; and if the space, or quadrangle, between the Lines of Head and Heart is narrow, a lack of confidence and rather serious outlook on life is likely. If the curve of the Line of Life is not wide but close to the thumb, it further compounds a cautious and perhaps fearful personality. When this combination of lines is found on the left hand, whilst the right hand shows the Lines of Head and Life with a shorter tie to them at their beginnings, early influences or parental attitudes will not have been conducive to creating self-certainty, but feelings of boldness and self-confidence will eventually be forthcoming to some extent. All the same, there will always be a basic wariness and some fundamental caution. Here, you would examine the Finger of Jupiter ♃ on each hand: if longer on the right, it will further promote self-esteem in adult life.

Whichever line on the palm is deepest and most clearly defined will be the line of most strength and effect in the personality. The line that is weakest and most delicately etched on the palm will be the one that is less energized. If the Line of Head is the finest line and sweeps steeply towards the wrist, it will correspond with a very imaginative mind, maybe too much so. The imagination will not be tempered by rational thinking and the inner world of fantasy can overlap into the external world of reality. There will be enormous sensitivity and if such a delicate line is found on both hands, the grip on reality will not be very firm. Prolific dreams and day-dreams are likely. For such a sensitive soul, early life can be especially difficult, as we are at our most vulnerable when we are children. Even if family influences are loving and kind, experiences such as going to school can be dramatic. A child with both Lines of Head like this will need lots of understanding.

If the Line of Head is straight for most of its length, but towards its end suddenly dips towards the Mount of the Moon ☽ (see below), the thinking will tend to be quite practical, but at the same time in touch with the imagination. Creative abilities may be dormant and therefore need recognition and encouragement. Sometimes this sort of line creates the ability to 'switch off' the mind and to relax in the realms of the imagination with ease. If this curve is found under the Finger of the Sun ☉, it is likely that it will be possible for the owner of such a hand to be in touch — maybe at a more unconscious level — with positive inner resources and energies. Sometimes it can also indicate the useful ability to 'cat nap' and feel quickly restored, especially mentally.

Like the other lines, the Line of Head changes. It can reflect worries, but it can also develop and extend itself. For example, a person who begins to study something that stretches his or her thinking and finds what is being learned interesting and mentally challenging, could find his or her Line of Head growing longer, extending from its former point of termination to reach down towards the outer edge of the palm. Someone who has a very finely etched Line of Head may easily feel taxed and depleted on a mental level. If some sort of mental discipline or course of study is taken up, and the mind is applied to it gently and with consistent regularity, it is possible that the mind and thinking processes will grow stronger. It may become less prone to fatigue and the memory, if poor, will improve. This will soon be evident on the Line of Head itself, which will grow stronger and more defined.

If we do not exercise our body enough, we lose muscle tone and lack energy. The same principle applies to the mind. We are far less likely to become senile in our later years if we keep our brain active throughout our life.

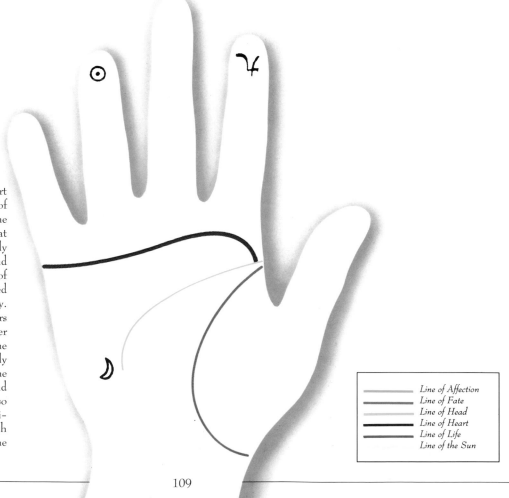

Right. When the Line of Heart dips under the Finger of Jupiter ♃ to merge with the Line of Head, it shows that emotional influences in early life were not easy to contend with and have created a lot of anger, which could be directed towards oneself or the family. If this line formation appears on both palms, hurt and anger will be especially marked. The Line of Head dips suddenly towards the Mount of the Moon ☽, indicating a mind that is practical but can also literally 'dip down' into imaginative, creative thinking. Such a line can belong to someone with a creative hobby.

	Line of Affection
	Line of Fate
	Line of Head
	Line of Heart
	Line of Life
	Line of the Sun

DEPRESSION AND ANXIETY

All of us are likely to experience depression at some time in our life. This can manifest on the palm in various ways. The Finger and Mount of Saturn ♄, together with the Line of Head, are the prime indicators of depression and anxious states.

A person who is predisposed to depression and gloom will often have a developed Mount of Saturn ♄ (see below). The Finger of the Sun ☉ may look weak or bend towards the Finger of Saturn. If tiny criss-cross bars are to be found on a high Mount of Saturn, a tendency to negative attitudes may be marked. Minor marks such as these can fade out, however, according to life's circumstances; their appearances on the mount may correspond with a temporary period of difficulty in life.

If the space between the Lines of Head and Heart is narrow, especially beneath the Finger of Saturn ♄ (see below left), then a narrow focus and a limited perspective can literally render worries more acute and difficult to deal with. Someone with these features who can otherwise cope with life quite effectively may find problems difficult to contend with. He or she may feel 'stuck' with worries while they exist and find it difficult to imagine better times forthcoming. Imaginative, sensitive types with a sloping Line of Head are more prone to depression than people with linear, straight, rational lines.

When depression occurs, always take into account the physical energies, as depletion and tiredness will make challenges more difficult to

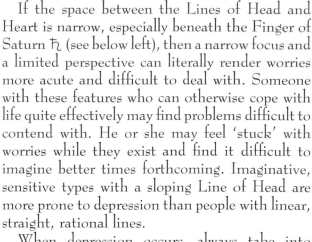

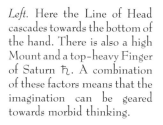

Left. Here the Line of Head cascades towards the bottom of the hand. There is also a high Mount and a top-heavy Finger of Saturn ♄. A combination of these factors means that the imagination can be geared towards morbid thinking.

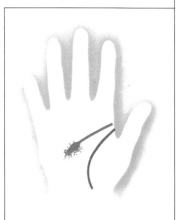

Above. Depression of a temporary kind is often revealed by a change in skin tone at the end of the Line of Head. It will actually be darker, almost like a little shadow clouding the horizon of thought while the depressive mood prevails.

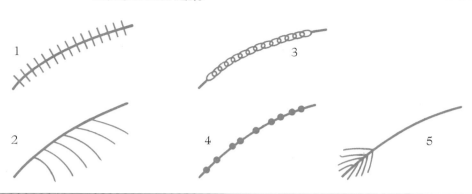

Right. There are various special marks on the Line of Head that can reveal temporary problems. 1. Crossbars show a time of anxiety. 2. Fine descending lines mean temporary depression. 3. Chains indicate weakness and vacillation. 4. Dots show debility and nervous problems. 5. Tassels reveal poor focus or memory.

respond to and problems can get out of perspective. Note the general tone of the hand. If there is little resilience to gentle fingertip pressure (especially in the centre of the palm, just below the Line of Heart and the Finger of Mercury ☿) energy levels may be low. Fine horizontal lines on the fingertips also indicate fatigue (see page 110, main illustration). When such signs are present, rest would be advisable.

Extreme anxiety over minor issues is often experienced by people with defined, knotty middle and upper finger joints. A tendency to be very analytical and fussy about everything can promote unnecessary worrying. If the space between the Lines of Head and Heart is narrow, then the knotty-fingered type may find it hard to take life lightly because a sense of humour may also be in short supply.

A strong looking Finger of the Sun ☉ (in relation to the other fingers) helps a person to be in touch with positive energies. A Line of the Sun furthers the ability to feel happy and optimistic.

Depression is often caused by feelings of anger or frustration that have not been expressed. If anger is internalized, then an emotional implosion can occur, leading to depression. People with a short Finger of Mercury ☿ may find it difficult to express their feelings verbally. If the Line of Head has tiny red patches on it, the owner is highly likely to have something on his or her mind that is creating inner anger. He or she should therefore be encouraged to bring the feelings out into the open and not let them simmer into depressive moods. Writing down feelings, just for one's own sake and well-being, can be a valuable means of externalizing anger.

The Mount of the Moon ☽ is linked to our moods. When the Line of Head slopes steeply into it, depression can occur. This mount also connects with the imagination; if it is full, on a hand with a pronounced Finger and Mount of Saturn ♄, the imagination is prone to deep fears and fantasies.

Do take special care when examining the hands of someone with depressive tendencies. Always bear in mind that the lines and minor markings can change. Finger and palm shapes do not change, however, but there is usually something that can be done to improve a predisposed tendency to depression or anxiety. There is a wide variety of conventional and alternative therapies to choose from.

Some people are so pre-programmed to worry about everything that if every source of anxiety were magically removed, they would still find something to worry about. It is possible to create problems unconsciously. Most of us do not live in the present: we tend to look back, often with guilt and remorse, or look forward with trepidation. If we review our past experiences from time to time, we can realize that the difficulties and crises we have to contend with now are often no more unmanageable than ones we have tackled in the past. Life goes on, nothing lasts forever and through dealing with problems, we learn to develop.

Do not be ashamed of an occasional depression. When you do feel a bit low, it is often easy to imagine you are the only one who gets fed up. Remember that we all feel down sometimes and that blue moods make the happy times better.

—————— Line of Affection	—————— Line of Heart
—————— Line of Fate	—————— Line of Life
—————— Line of Head	Line of the Sun

PRESSURE AND TRAUMA

Modern life puts us all under considerable pressure. Some of us cannot take the stress and tension and suffer from nervous afflictions or even breakdowns. A very high percentage of people need help from a psychiatrist, psychologist or counsellor at some point in life. Your palms can help by showing when things are getting on top of you, before the pressure or unhappiness begins to manifest in obvious ways.

Firstly, take an overview of the palm. If there are many lines on it, this indicates a great deal of nervous activity; whereas if the palm has few lines, the whole system, especially the nervous system, will be far less active and therefore not as vulnerable.

Those with elementary hands are very unlikely ever to crack under strain as they tend not to be too sensitive to things generally and are able to take things in their stride. Square-handed types will often find practical ways of dealing with life. Although they can still be very sensitive, they are not as prone to being overwhelmed by pressure as other types. Pointed and conic hands are usually more vulnerable, particularly if the hands are also thin. If knotty fingers are in evidence as well, the owner is almost certain to be terribly over-sensitive.

Above. A fragile Line of Head. The tiny cross-lines and dots show a tendency to suffer from pressure headaches.

Above. A broken Line of Head shows too much pressure, weakening the mind.

Pressure and trauma, if severe, will reflect on the whole hand, but on the Line of Head in particular. If this line is more delicate looking, thinner and finer than the others, the mental responses will be sensitive and it will be most important to have enough rest and to try to externalize and deal with any anxiety before pressures build up and deplete the mind.

Headaches are caused by pressure and worry (unless there is a physical reason for them). Migraines can show on the Line of Head as fine little lines crossing over it, or as tiny dots, as if the line had been pricked by a pin (see top right). The deeper the little cross-lines or indentations on the line, the more severe the headaches are likely to be. If you find that these marks phase out on the line, the problem is likely to be of a temporary nature.

Major breakdown can actually manifest as a broken Line of Head.

Little 'sister' lines can often be found overlapping the ends of the break above or below it, helping to carry the owner through a difficult period (see right, second illustration down). A less severe crisis can show when the Line of Head, though not breaking, has a thinner, finer portion on it. A star on the Line of Head can also indicate a big shock to the mind and nervous system, but if there is also a square on the Line of Head, close to or covering the star, it suggests the ability to recover quickly (see right, third illustration down). Squares found anywhere on the palm are always protective and helpful signs. A star at the end of the Line of Head has a more crucial meaning than one found elsewhere on this line, especially when found on a line that slopes steeply towards the wrist. In such cases it indicates severe problems of a deeper psychological nature than sudden shock.

Above. The star on this steeply sloping Line of Head shows a shock that registers both mentally and physically.

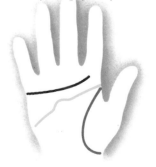

Above. A slight curve in this Line of Head shows great strain; but it is overcome.

Once again, remember to look at both hands. You may find, for example, that a thin, fine and vulnerable Line of Head on the left hand has more definition on the right. This means that although the owner is very sensitive on a mental level, he or she will start to find things easier to cope with as time goes by.

A period of great strain that does not culminate in breakdown can be revealed by a slight curve or bend in the Line of Head in an upwards direction (see bottom right). If the curve is not blotchy or red, difficulties shall be borne well and overcome, but with enormous effort.

Chains on the Line of Head line running the length of the line can indicate a physical condition that affects the thinking processes (see far right). There may be lassitude and a corresponding inability to deal easily with the pressures of life.

The mind and the body reflect each other. If there is a physical problem or lack of energy, then everything will be harder to handle on a mental level. Likewise, if there is a lot of mental stress to contend with, it will deplete the body and its reserves of energy. The colour of the Line of Head can reveal much about stress. If it is redder than the other lines, particularly if there are also tiny red spots on it, then there may be some situation in the person's life that is a source of pressure, anger and frustration. Small, dark spots mean heavy worries that temporarily and intensely take up a lot of thinking space. As the worry lifts, the dark or red spots will disappear.

A sloping Line of Head always indicates sensitive thinking. The steeper the slope, the greater the degree of sensitivity and imagination there will be. A very steep line can create a tendency to over-worry, to let the imagination run amok, magnifying pressures and trauma in a disproportionate manner. When any spots, chains or breaks are found on such a Line of Head, the ability to realize perspective, or to regain equilibrium after any trauma, will always take longer than for someone with a straighter Line of Head, who is likely to be more rational.

If the hands are hard-skinned, lack flexibility and the thumb is stiff and unyielding, there can be a tendency not to 'give in' to pressures, and to battle on when there has been some trauma or major upset. At times of crisis, we sometimes have to be strong, but it is also important to acknowledge our needs and feelings and not to hide them beneath a stubborn mask of strength. This can lay a store of future difficulty when the pressure can no longer be ignored and needs to be faced up to and dealt with.

If the mind has had much to contend with, the memory can temporarily become diffused and vague. A great shock can also fragment the memory for a time. Whilst the trauma encompasses the thinking processes, the mind may choose to remember pleasant influences, and attempt to block out less pleasing recollections. This will be reflected on the palm as a blurred area at the end of the Line of Head. When the shock lifts, the line becomes clear again.

When carrying out a reading, always be particularly tactful if it appears that someone is undergoing a traumatic period.

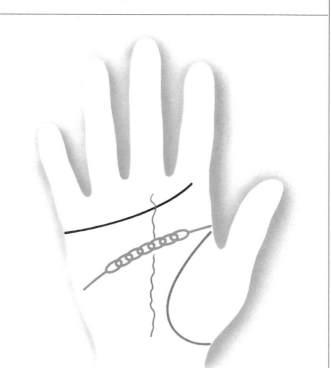

	Line of Affection		Line of Heart
	Line of Fate		Line of Life
	Line of Head		Line of the Sun

Above. Chains on the Line of Head imprison the thinking and behaviour in moodiness and mental malaise. Note that the Line of Fate is weak, indicating that unbalanced mental pressure and energy will make life difficult.

THE ROAD TO RECOVERY

When we are going through a critical period in our lives, through illness, emotional upsets or problems with career or money, it is often difficult to realize that nothing lasts forever and that most problems improve or are eventually resolved. If they do not, we can always learn to make the best of the situation.

As we have seen, the left hand reveals basic tendencies and the right shows future events. When you are looking at the hands of someone who is going through a time of difficulty, note very carefully the differences between the hands in order to ascertain when more positive influences will be forthcoming. In so doing, you can encourage a more forward-looking attitude.

When you are looking at the hands of a person who, for some reason, is not very happy, you may find that he or she needs to talk about whatever is causing a disturbance in their lives. If this happens, be patient and allow for any need to externalize a difficulty through talking to you about it. When we do not express what is bothering or worrying us, the problem can be magnified, grow out of perspective and then worsen. A trouble shared is a trouble halved, as they say.

Most counsellors are sought out because they are there not only to help and advise, but also to listen in an objective, understanding and non-judgemental way. If you think about it, it is rather sad that so many people have to pay in order to be met with understanding. This book will not make you a counsellor, but if you are going to attempt to read anyone's hands, you must also be prepared to listen, especially if you are going to glean any intimate, personal details about the life of a person who puts trust in your observations. Be discreet, too, not allowing your observations to be a source of gossip. Share any problems and then keep them to yourself. We reap what we sow, so bear this in mind and use whatever you may learn from this book with integrity.

The road to recovery after an emotional, physical or mental trauma, or indeed any period of difficulty, will show on the line that is associated with whatever has happened. If there has been a crisis affecting the mind, for example, take special note of the Line of Head. If there is a disturbance on it, as shown by bars crossing the line (see left), islands, breaks or dots on the left hand, whilst the line on the right hand is clear, you will be able to say that the problems are of a temporary nature and that things will return to normal.

If there is an island on the Line of Heart on the left hand but not on the right, a critical time emotionally will soon be healed and belong to the past. If the line on both hands is not strong in comparison to other lines, recovery from a time of difficulty will take a bit longer than otherwise. The heart is the seat of emotions and registers how we feel. Islands can sometimes reflect a weak heart, which may not be able to take too much stress.

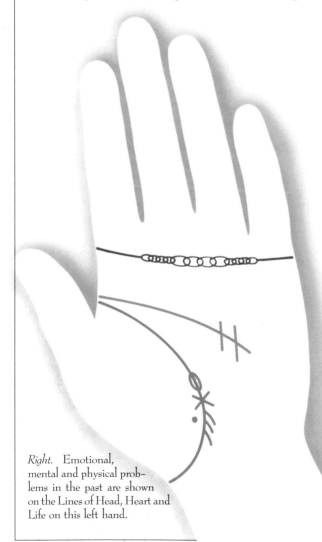

Right. Emotional, mental and physical problems in the past are shown on the Lines of Head, Heart and Life on this left hand.

This does not necessarily mean that the owner has a life-threatening condition, but that energy on a general level may not be very forthcoming, in which case medical help should be sought and rest would be wise.

The Line of Fate is very important in terms of showing change and renewal. When it breaks or fragments, it always indicates a great change. Most of us fear change, although it is often what we need. Depending on our state of inner security and confidence, a time of transition will usually be, at best, anticipated with some trepidation. If we are not positively attuned to life, looming changes can feel threatening and cause much fear and anxiety. When you think about the fact that people can be very upset just by moving house, you realize just how vulnerable and fearful some of us are.

A new beginning will also be reflected in the Line of Fate when it starts anew after a break. Squares or 'sister' lines are helpful influences that can protect a break or act as a bridge between one set of conditions and another.

Renewal and recovery after illness will show on the Line of Life. Past surgical operations will often be revealed by a tiny pinprick indentation on, or just inside, the Line of Life. On the right, the corresponding place on the line will have grown stronger.

The thumb can tell a lot about strength of character and will. A weak, short thumb on the hand of someone who has experienced some suffering, shows that he or she does not find it easy to exert their will. In this case, you could encourage the owner to try to be stronger. If a weak thumb is accompanied by a high Mount of Saturn ♄ and a Line of Fate that runs right up into the lower section of the Finger of Saturn, it can reveal a life that is more heavily fated than most. Conditions in life can be unavoidably difficult and it may be hard to muster a positive outlook.

We often create our own problems. Many people find it very difficult to learn from past mistakes. They keep on repeating negative patterns of behaviour, even though their quality of life suffers as a result. But some people seem almost blind to the root cause of their troubles. Features to watch out for are stiff, unyielding hands and thumbs, a narrow space between the Lines of Head and Heart and a raised Mount of Mars ♂. All these can contribute to a dogged refusal to accept one's shortcomings or negative patterns and to attempt to change them. A high Mount of Jupiter ♃ can further such attitudes through pride. When used positively, however, these qualities can be excellent in promoting determination.

We are not merely victims of fate, though for some of us fate is less kind than for others. As human beings, however, we all have, to some degree, the ability to direct and create our own destiny according to our will-power, faith and outlook on life.

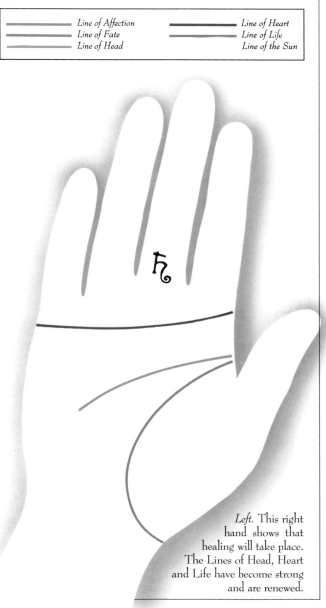

Line of Affection		Line of Heart
Line of Fate		Line of Life
Line of Head		Line of the Sun

Left. This right hand shows that healing will take place. The Lines of Head, Heart and Life have become strong and are renewed.

NECESSARY TENSIONS

Above. This Mount of Mercury ☿ is noticeably flatter than the other mounts, which reveals a lack of impetus that may be linked to low levels of nervous or mental energy. Very narrow nails and a palm with little bounce or resilience will further an unenergetic response to life. The Line of Head is short and straight, indicating a rather dull mind.

Above. This Line of Heart is chained along its length and there is a very wide space between it and the Line of Head. This shows laziness.

Although a great many of us live with rather too much tension and anxiety, we all need a certain amount to provide our impetus for achieving and creating something in life. Like everything else, it is all a question of balance. We should ideally be able to access our inner dynamic forces that can create positive, well-directed energy, while also being able to relax and restore ourselves in readiness for the next phase of activity.

A lack of impetus can create problems. Its causes can be manifold. Boredom, weariness, depression or some physical imbalance can wither the will to do much. When little is achieved as a result, whatever caused the inertia in the first place can worsen. A downward-spiral influence can come into effect making the very spark of life dull and lack-lustre.

The hand shows when there is too much tension or not enough. Although a person may be predisposed to either extreme, there is usually something that can be done to create a more balanced situation. Too much tension can be revealed by a stiff hand with a hard palm that does not 'give' when gently prodded with your fingertips. The palm may also be very red and look as if

it has been pumped up, rather like a balloon that, if inflated any further, would burst. When these factors are all found, there will be an inability to relax and let go. Even when the owner appears to be resting, a high level of internal activity will still be generated. Sometimes a physical condition linked to the blood pressure can be a major contributory factor to such behaviour. It is possible to cure or at least calm this condition through medication and a change in diet and life-style.

When people hold their thumbs clenched inside a fist, it can reveal a tense disposition. It can also literally reflect a 'tight-fisted' or mean disposition, which could stem from a fear of letting go, materially or otherwise.

If the palm has a Simian Line (see A Law Unto Themselves, pages 90-91), as well as the aforementioned features, the internal pressure can be acute. If the thumb is bulbous, the inability to handle extreme tensions may present a source of great difficulty.

A lack of necessary tension and impetus can be revealed on a palm that is very maleable and soft with a lot of 'give' under gentle fingertip pressure. The fingers may bend away from the palm very readily. If the skin and the lines on the palm are pale, there could be a physical condition that needs to be investigated, which may be linked to blood pressure or the quality of the blood.

Some people are naturally lazy and do not worry about it. They like to lounge through life without too much difficulty. In such cases, the palm will be smooth and soft. A small, weak thumb and rounded fingertips show that will-power may be lacking. If the outer edge of the palm does not curve and the Mounts of Mars ♂ are not pronounced, there will be little internal pressure to galvanize much productive activity. A weak or missing Line of Fate will compound any tendencies to just float through life. A long tie be-tween the Lines of Head and Life could, in this case, amplify a lack of independence.

If most, or all, of the lines on the palm are chained, particularly the Line of Head, vacillation and a lack of defined and dynamic response to life may be linked to some major physical imbalance. In such cases, it is a good idea to suggest gently

that the person whose palms you are reading goes for a general medical check-up. As always, be careful not to worry people unnecessarily.

Fear can be an enormous stumbling block for some people and inhibit action. People fear failure, but success too. The Finger of Jupiter ♃ is linked to ambition, confidence and self-esteem. If this finger is short on both hands, an inability to generate much positive, forward-moving dynamic energy may stem from a basic lack of self-confidence.

People with elementary hands often have very similar right and left hands, indicating a steady, anxiety-free course through life, not buffeted much by the winds of change. The hand may be firm and energetic and, to the untrained eye, may seem rather stiff and tense. Remember that the basic, simplistic hand does not usually belong to one who experiences much nervous tension. The energies here are prompted by basic survival needs. At the end of a hard day's work, this type is likely to be able to relax and sleep like a log.

Right. A Simian Line (see pages 90-91) together with a high Mount of Mars ♂ found at the beginning of the Line of Life indicates great tension. A cross below the Mount of Jupiter ♃ can mean that ten-sion may erupt unreasonably. This type will need to have a very defined means of chan-nelling energies constructively.

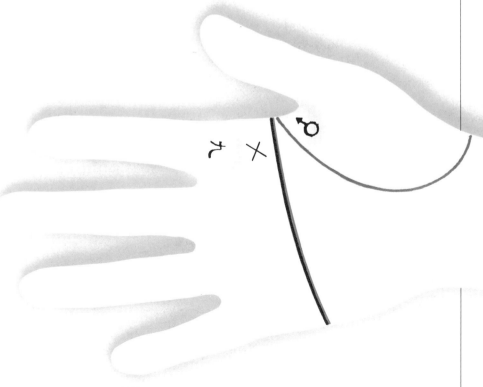

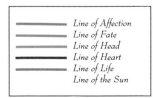

Line of Affection
Line of Fate
Line of Head
Line of Heart
Line of Life
Line of the Sun

ACCIDENTS, ADDICTION AND LIFE-STYLE

We all have accidents from time to time, but why is it that some people are accident-prone? Similarly, many of us would admit to being 'addicted' to something to a certain extent, such as cigarettes, alcohol, or even tea or coffee. But why is it that addiction takes over the lives of some people? Our health – physical and mental – can be adversely affected by our life-style, yet it is often our attitude to life that brings about such problems. Here we will find out how the hand can reveal a tendency to bring problems on oneself, and look at the possible underlying causes.

Accidentally on Purpose?

Some people are more accident-prone than others, but the reasons for being so can be more complex than clumsiness or lack of co-ordina-tion. It is interesting to realize that we often unconsciously create mishaps or accidents through our own actions. Accidents often occur when there are difficulties or worrying conditions in our lives, when we are in need of some attention, or perhaps rest and some respite from stress, overwork or tedium.

Crosses on the Line of Life on the right hand can mean a possible future accident. If a cross is protected by a square, however, the severity will always be reduced. This is especially so when the Line of Life on the left hand is strong and clear. A cross on the Line of Head can mean an accident to the head or eyes, and here too, if there is a square surrounding the cross, it will serve to protect the owner from danger and promote healing.

Major mishaps frequently happen when we are on holiday or enjoying a sporting activity such as skiing or climbing. If a cross is found on a Line of Travel on the right hand, it would be a good idea to postpone travelling to other countries until the cross fades from the line, or to try to avoid potentially dangerous situations.

The Addictive Palm

'A little of what you fancy does you good,' as they say. But moderation is difficult for some of us. When something feels good, we may want more, until a craving sets in, leading to addiction.

People who have difficulty controlling their cravings often have a Line of Addiction. This is found running from the Line of Life, curving up towards the centre of the palm, then drooping to the Mount of the Moon ☽. Be careful not to confuse this line with a Line of Travel or a Line of Affection, both of which emanate from the Line of Life. If this line is found on both palms, there

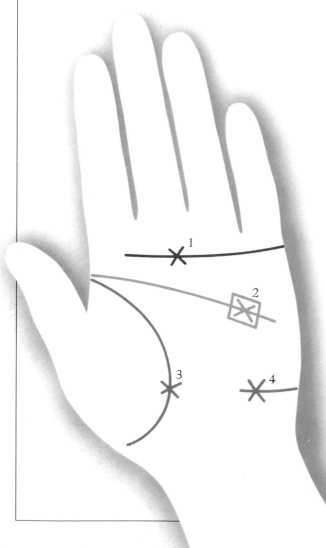

Left. Accidents are often linked to crosses on the lines. 1. The cross on the Line of Heart often means an emotional blow or disappointment. 2. On the Line of Head it can reveal an accident affecting the head or eyes. 3. On the Line of Life a cross can mean an acci-dent to the body. 4. Found on a Line of Travel a cross can indicate a mishap or accident whilst travelling. When a square is found covering a cross on any line, it always helps to reduce the seriousness of the injury, and to promote healing and renewal.

may be a habitual tendency to over-indulge in alcohol, drugs or other addictive substances. In such cases, addictions can be more difficult to overcome. When this is the case, a Line of Mercury is likely to be found as well. On the hand of an addict, it is usually unclear and broken as it courses up the palm towards the Mount of Mercury ☿. If the thumb is small and weak and the palm as a whole is soft, the ability to be sufficiently strong-willed to overcome bad habits may be lacking. If the Line of Addiction is found on the left hand only, the addictive tendency may have been modified or the owner might be outgrowing it. If found on the right hand, the Line of Addiction reveals that the urge to use drugs or drink frequently may be a passing or controllable phase. This is because there is no basic tendency to hedonism.

A Flexible Outlook

We all need a framework to our lives. A certain amount of routine gives us a sense of order. Some people, however, get so stuck in their patterns of behaviour that the structure of their lives becomes restrictive.

A tendency towards very fixed attitudes and corresponding patterns of behaviour is revealed on the palm in various ways: an inflexible palm; a straight thumb with no discernible 'waist' between the upper and lower phalanges; fingers that do not bend away from the palm under slight pressure; a short or absent Line of the Sun; and a Line of Fate etched heavily onto the palm. If the skin on the palm is hard and dry, there will be an inclination not to relax easily. People with hard-skinned palms will generally be so disposed towards constant, relentless activity that any encouragement to 'let go' a bit will be ignored. It is often fear, which can manifest in our lives in so many ways, that causes a reluctance to change what is familiar and certain. For some people, repetitive patterns of behaviour can represent security. A straight Line of Head can mean a limited imagination: which can make behaviour patterns even more crystallized. When these features are found on both palms, their effects are amplified.

Fixed attitudes and patterns of behaviour can create physical problems. There are many illnesses that are directly linked to a rigid approach to life, such as some arthritic, back, and even heart conditions. When you are presented with a hand with the above characteristics, you could gently enquire about the subject's life-style. If there is a tendency or need to stick to very defined patterns, you could suggest that a good way to experience a fuller, and probably better way of being would be to try to break some of the self-imposed rules.

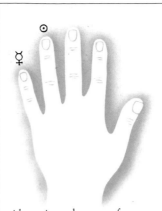

Above. An indication of struggle, especially in early life, can be seen on a hand with low-set Fingers of Mercury ☿ and the Sun ☉. When the fingers are set on the hand in a straight line, it can mean that benefits come more readily.

Below. The Line of Addiction arches across the palm from the Line of Life to the Mount of the Moon ☽.

	Line of Affection		Line of Heart
	Line of Fate		Line of Life
	Line of Head		Line of the Sun

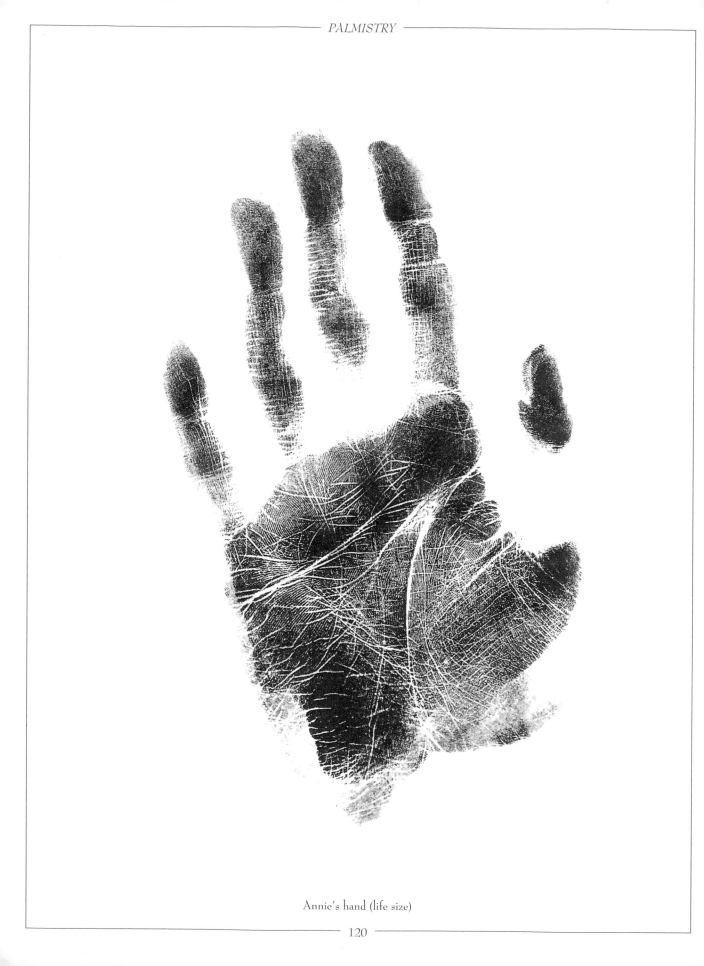

Annie's hand (life size)

SAMPLE READING
ANNIE'S HAND

Annie is right-handed. This is her left hand, which reveals her past and her basic tendencies. The first thing you probably will notice is the fine network of lines all over the palm. This indicates that Annie is very sensitive with a highly active nervous system.

Annie had health problems from a very early age, which are reflected on the palm. She was born three months premature and was lucky to survive. When a baby is growing in the womb, the eyes are one of the last parts to develop fully. As Annie was so premature, she had to be put into an incubator. She was not expected to live, and was given too much oxygen, which severely damaged her weak, unfortunate underdeveloped eyes. As a result, she became ninety per cent blind in the left eye and sixty-five per cent blind in the right. Look carefully at the Line of Head. It splits at the end and the branches form an elongated island that actually resembles the shape of an eye. This reveals her disability, which is worse in her left eye and is thus reflected on the left hand.

From the ages of two to five, she underwent several eye operations. Look at the Line of Head again. Near the beginning of the line, before the eye-shaped island, there are several blurred pin-prick indentations, which actually correspond with each operation. Whenever a person has a surgical operation, it will be revealed on the palm in this way. If it is found close to the Line of Life, an operation on the body is indicated. When it is found on the Line of Head, as in Annie's case, surgery to the head or eyes is revealed.

As a child, Annie suffered a great deal. Deeply sensitive, she lived in a half-lit world, often feeling alienated and misunderstood. Had she been born totally blind, in a strange way things may have been easier for her; but, having partial sight made her feel clumsy and afraid of what she could not see. These factors, together with having to be hospitalized frequently, would have been difficult for any child, but for one so sensitive, it was dreadful. As she was not expected to live and could not be held and nursed immediately after her birth, the bonding process between mother and child did not happen. This might explain why her mother was very cool and critical, and often not very encouraging or sympathetic towards her daughter.

The operations did help the rather fragile little girl. Her sight improved greatly. She began to come into her own when she went to a special school, finding comfort in being with other partially sighted children. Even though she no longer felt so different and alienated from others, it took a while longer for her to feel less threatened by the outside world that she had been unable to see clearly for so many years. Look at the Mount of Jupiter. Like the Mount of Mars, it is well developed. These mounts helped Annie to find growing confidence and strength within herself. Her Line of the Sun helped to further her creative perceptions and optimism.

Annie is now forty, and a social worker. She works with drug addicts and has a lot of responsibility. Previously, she worked with mentally-ill people. She really cares about others. Perhaps because she has suffered so much, she can empathize with the problems and weaknesses of others. She has a real talent for drawing, shown in her sloping Line of Head and good Line of the Sun, which she is finding great pleasure in developing. Annie has achieved and overcome much, and is therefore to be admired.

COMMON QUESTIONS

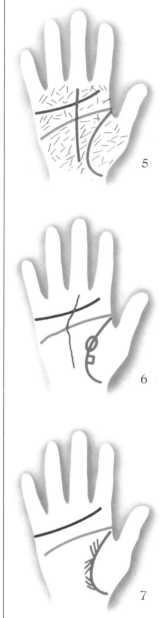

1. My Line of Life looks short. Does that mean that my life will be short as well?
   Your Line of Life literally moves away from what is familiar. Life will go on, but in a totally new place.

2. I drink a lot because I have a stressful job. Could this be the reason why I often have no energy and feel run-down and negative?
   You have a line branching from your Line of Life that indicates a dependence. Your lack of energy is due to the high levels of toxins in your body. Try to be moderate and you will feel better.

3. Why do I get very depressed sometimes, even when things are going well?
   Your Line of Head slopes, showing a creative, imaginative and sensitive nature, which is also prone to depression. Accept how you are and realize that most people feel down sometimes.

4. I have a mark that looks like a star on my Line of Head. What does this mean?
   This mark suggests you need plenty of sleep. Try to avoid stress and deal with anxiety promptly.

5. Why do my hands perspire so much?
   Your palms are very lined, which means that your disposition may be nervous. Antiperspirants can inhibit perspiration on the body's trunk and create a tendency to do so through the hands or feet.

6. There is an island on my right hand's Line of Life. Does this mean I will be ill?
   If you do become ill, it will not be serious as you have a square covering the island that will lend strength and speed recovery.

7. I am usually full of energy and enthusiasm. Why have I recently started to feel tired and depleted?
   Your Line of Life has some little lines descending from it, indicating temporary problems. The rising lines, however, mean that you will soon be on top form again.

8. I seem to have two Lines of Life. What does this mean?
   The Line of Mars, running alongside your Line of Life, acts as a buffer against illness as it brings great vitality and a fighting spirit.

9. I have had migraines for the past four years. Will they disappear?
   There are tiny crossbars on your Line of Head, which correspond with anxiety or headaches. As they phase out, you will outgrow them.

10. I cannot concentrate and my memory is unreliable at the moment. Why is this?

There is some diffusion at the end of your Line of Head affecting your thinking. There is also an island, which indicates a temporary taxing of your mind.

11. I know I overeat. My husband says I am too fat. I feel ugly but keep eating, sometimes secretly. Why is this?

The underlying reason may be linked to your marriage as your Line of Affection does not look happy. It forks and dips to your Line of Heart. You may need help. Counselling might be a good idea.

12. I have very painful and debilitating periods. Does this show on my hands?

Your first rascette curves up in the middle. This can correspond with a minor problem, as can the island on your Line of Life. See your doctor and sort it out.

13. I have arthritis in my knees and back. Friends have suggested acupuncture but I am suspicious of alternative medicine. Would it be good for me?

You have a very narrow quadrangle (the space between your Lines of Head and Heart), which can mean blinkered attitudes. Try whatever is available to improve your health. The arthritic condition is creating lassitude and general debility, shown by hair lines drooping from the Line of Life.

14. I do not like sex very much but would like to fall in love and overcome my reticence.

Your lower Line of Affection curves up on the Mount of Mercury ☿, which can indicate celibacy, or extreme romantic discernment. Another line above, however, shows a happy, mutually fulfilling union.

15. I spend at least four hours a day exercising, yet I cannot relax easily. Why is this?

Your Simian Line indicates intensity of focus and energy. Be fit, but do not let it become an obsession. What else interests you?

16. My wife has to undergo major surgery. I love her so much. Will she be OK?

The small dot on your Line of Affection shows her illness. But the line continues normally, showing that you will both be feeling fine soon. Be strong and supportive for her.

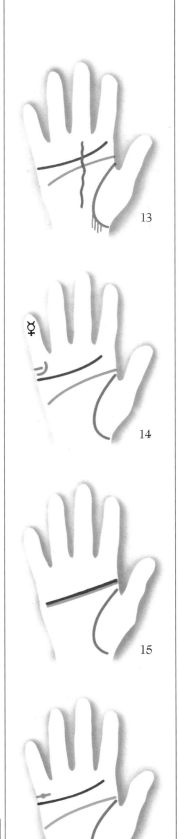

9

13

10

14

11

15

12

	Line of Affection		Line of Heart
	Line of Fate		Line of Life
	Line of Head		Line of the Sun

16

Afterword

Now that you have learned the basics of palmistry, where do you go from here? You are probably impatient to read and apply your budding skills, but naturally you will want to do things properly and to the best of your ability. Like anything of value, acquiring the art of palmistry takes time, patience and plenty of practice.

Observation

The best way to begin is to observe people's hands at every opportunity. Wherever you are — in the supermarket, on the bus, at a party — pay attention to hand shapes, gesticulations, lines and features. You can even learn a lot from looking at the hands of people on television. Becoming a full-time hand-watcher will benefit your palmistry skills enormously. Does your bank manager have business-like, square hands? Does your daughter's art teacher have conic, creative hands? Does your neurotic neighbour have very pointed fingers?

As you observe and learn, keep this book by your side, turning to the relevant pages as often as you need to. It is also a good idea to record your observations in a notebook. This will help you to register in your memory the information in this book. As the hands change with time, a written record of a reading can be very interesting to consult later when you read the same person's hands again. People sometimes forget parts of a reading, and are fascinated when you remind them of what was said. An observation that seemed minor at the time may now, in retrospect, have marked the start of a new, important phase. There *is* a lot to remember, so do not get disheartened.

Application

It is best if you have a *modus operandi,* a step-by-step approach to reading the palms. Use the following steps as a guide:
1. Identify the shape of the hands and fingers.
2. Assess the tone, resilience and flexibility of the hands and fingers.
3. Note any major differences between the right and left hands.
4. Look at each of the mounts.
5. Examine each of the major lines individually, choosing a sequence that suits you.
6. Look at the way the major lines interact.
7. What are the minor lines saying?
8. Try and interpret any other, more unusual features.

Illumination

With patience and practice, you will gradually become familiar with the lines and features on the palm and their meanings. This stage is very exciting, because it liberates your mind from concentrating on remembering everything you have learned and your intuitive senses start to come to the fore. As you focus on the palm, you are quite likely to begin 'picking up' mental imagery or impressions about the other person. Places, buildings, people and sometimes even names may float across your inner field of vision. This shows that you are now at the level of carrying out an intimate palm reading. As you progress, you will find that more and more subtle sources of information filter through from your unconscious and from that of the person whose palms you are reading. A peaceful, quiet and comfortable setting will enhance the possibility of your intuitive abilities working for you.

I hope that you have enjoyed reading this book as much as I have enjoyed writing it, and that you will continue to further your knowledge of this ancient and fascinating study of human nature.

INDEX

A

academic ability 60-1, 73
accidents 118
acrobats 53
actors 52-3, 72
adaptability 93
addiction 118-19
affairs 78-9, 88-9, 95
aggression 90
alcohol 119, 122
allergies 103
ambition 21-47
anaemia 100, 104
anxiety 39, 110-11, 122
architects 58
arthritis 119, 123
artistic hand 50-1, 73
athletes 63

B

back problems 104-5, 119
bladder problems 103
bowel problems 103
breakdown 112-13
broad hands 11
broken heart 92-3
bumps 33, 53, 106

C

career 21-47
    changes and breaks 42-3
    family and 36-7
    questions 46-7
    sample reading 45
catarrh 103
celibacy 77, 123
chains 78, 79, 101, 103,
    108, 111, 117
charisma 29, 52
children 6, 37, 73, 86-7
closed hand 11
colour 100, 103, 113
comedians 53
compatibility 82-5
concentration 91
confidence 73, 82, 108, 121

congestion, head 103
conic fingers 14, 15, 71, 79,
    83, 107
conic hand 13, 24, 31, 52,
    112
creative ability 49-59
    questions 72-3
    sample reading 70-1
Creative Curve 10, 11
'croix mystique' see Cross of
    Intuition
Cross of Intuition 57, 67-9,
    71
crossbars 30, 31, 32, 33, 42,
    43, 46, 63, 102, 111,
    114
crosses 31, 36-7, 41, 42, 46,
    63, 77, 101, 118
Curve of Strength 11

D

dancers 53
death, predicting 39
demonstrative nature 81
depression 35, 73, 102,
    110-11, 122
development 34-5
diet, effect on hands 102-3
diplomacy 15, 67
dots 101, 104, 111, 112, 114
drugs, addiction to 119
dyspepsia 102

E

eczema 106
elementary hand 13, 24, 62,
    79, 83, 107, 112, 117
emotional problems 92-3,
    108-9
entrepreneurs 32-3
eyesight 106, 121

F

family 35
    career and 36-7

problems with 106, 107
Family Ring 41, 58
fatigue 107
fear 117, 119
fickleness 78-9
figure '8' 69
Finger of Jupiter (index) 14,
    26, 66-7, 117
    angle 16
    health indications 102,
        105
    length 31, 32, 36, 45, 47,
        52-3, 56, 71, 72, 82,
        108
    phalanges 18
    pointing with 10
    tip 62, 65, 66-7
Finger of Mercury (little) 14,
    26, 27, 33, 61
    angle 16, 31, 54
    bump on 53
    health indications 105
    knots 65
    length 111
    phalanges 18, 33, 45,
        52-3, 54, 61
Finger of Saturn (middle) 14
    angle 16
    health indications 105, 110
    length 32, 45
    phalanges 18, 56, 62, 64,
        69
    pointing with 10
    tip 58, 59, 61
Finger of the Sun (ring) 14,
    29
    angle 16
    health indications 105,
        110, 111
    length 31, 32, 45, 47, 53,
        61, 82, 83, 86
    phalanges 18
fingers,
    angles 16, 31
    bumps on pads 33, 53
    flexibility 11, 60, 67, 79,
        90
    health indications 102
    held together 10
    length 11, 12, 22, 26, 31,
        45, 71

phalanges 18
    horizontal lines on 100,
        107
    reading 14-15
    rubbing together 10
    setting 11, 119
    spaces between 11, 16, 31,
        32, 79, 82
    types 14, 15
fixed attitudes 119
flirtatiousness 95
food, effect on hands 102-3

G

generosity 83
gestures 10
Girdle of Venus 41, 50-1,
    71, 80, 93
gluttony 102
gourmet 102
gout 103
'green fingers' 62
grilles 35, 42, 47, 102-3

H

haemorrhoids 102
hand,
    colour 100
    gestures 10
    language 10-11
    sections 18
    shape 13, 26, 31, 107
    size 11
    strength 26
handshake 10
happiness 76-7
hard-skinned palms 83, 90,
    101
headaches 112, 122
healers 66-7
Healing Stigmata 66
health 6, 99-125
    questions 122-3
    sample reading 120-1
heart problems 104, 119
heart-break 92-3
helpers 66-7, 72

hollow palm 29, 77
humour, sense of 76-7, 85, 111
hypochondria 107

I

idealists 79
idolatry 93
independence 83
index finger see Finger of Jupiter
indigestion 102
inhibitions 108
intestinal disorders 103
introverted extrovert 53
intuitive signs 68-9
inventors 56-7
islands 30, 31, 42, 60, 73, 102-4, 107, 108, 114-15

J

jealousy 81, 84
job satisfaction 24-5

K

kidney problems 103
knotty joints 50, 56, 64-5, 111, 112

L

language of hands 10-11
large hands 11
lawyers 52-3, 72
laziness 116-17
leadership skills 26-7
left hand 12
life expectancy 6
life-style 119
Line of Addiction 118-19
Line of Affection 40-1, 47, 76, 78, 85, 88-9
breaks in 40, 84
dipping 85, 92-3, 123
forking 73, 88, 89, 123
meaning 88-9
multiple 40-1, 88-9, 123
positions 76, 89
touching other lines 93

Line of Ambition 23, 35, 53
Line of Destiny see Line of Fate
Line of Fate 6, 113
branching 22, 26, 35, 45, 46
breaks in 33, 42, 43, 92, 115
career and 22-30, 32, 33, 34, 35-46
creativity and 59, 71
crossbars on 33, 43, 46
direction to read 38
double 27, 43, 46
errant 27, 33
forking 23, 32, 40
health and 115
left and right compared 22-3, 59, 71
and Line of Life 36, 45, 59
lines drooping from 24
lines merging with 89
love and 89, 92
marks on 40, 41, 42, 46, 115
missing 22, 28, 117
position 22, 26-7, 32, 33, 36-7, 45, 115
'sister' lines 42, 115
terminating at Line of Heart 24, 25
time spans 38, 39
wavy 29, 35
Line of Head 76
academic ability and 60-1
branching 29, 52, 56, 57, 71, 72, 121
breaks in 112, 114
bumps on 106
career and 24, 27, 29, 32, 33, 35, 47
chains on 101, 103, 111, 113, 117
changes in 109
colour 113
combined with Line of Heart 39, 81, 90
compatibility and 85
creativity and 50, 51, 52, 53, 54, 56-7, 58, 71, 72-3
crossbars on 42, 111, 114
direction to read 38
erratic 51
forking 41, 54, 55, 61, 71, 72

health indications 103, 106, 110-15, 121
jealousy and 81
length 47, 60, 72, 117
and Line of Heart 53, 61, 85, 108, 109, 110, 115
and Line of Life 29, 32, 41, 51, 73, 79, 83, 85, 103, 108
lines from 71, 73, 111
love and 79, 85
marks on 35, 41, 42, 61, 73, 111, 112, 113, 114-15, 118, 121, 122
mental health and 108-9, 112-15
position 27, 35
quality 52, 57, 60-1, 85, 108
'sister' lines 112
sloping 29, 33, 50, 52, 53, 56, 58, 60, 71, 79, 81, 85, 108, 110, 111, 112
straight 24, 50, 53, 60, 61, 109, 117
Line of Heart 27
academic ability and 61
branching 79
chains on 78, 79, 104
combined with Line of Head 39, 81, 90
direction to read 38
feathery 84
healing and 66
health and 104-5, 114-15
length 66, 79, 81, 82, 84-5
and Line of Head 53, 61, 85, 108, 109, 110, 115
lines crossing 78
lines rising from 79
love and 76-85
marks on 104, 105, 114-15, 118
mental health and 108, 109
position 27, 80
quality 61
straight 61
wavy 78
Line of Influence 37, 40, 85, 89
Line of Intuition 45, 67, 68
Line of Life 6
aspects covered by 39

career and 23, 29, 32, 36, 42
creativity and 59
direction to read 38
health indications 106, 115
and Line of Fate 36, 45, 59
and Line of Head 29, 32, 41, 51, 73, 79, 83, 85, 103, 108
marks on 41, 42, 101, 106, 115, 118
mental health and 108
position 23
time spans 38
Line of Mars 40, 71, 122
Line of Mercury 101, 106-7, 119
Line of the Sun 121
breaks in 51
career and 23, 24, 25, 27, 28-33, 35, 37, 43, 45, 46-7
creativity and 51, 52, 54, 57, 59, 71, 72, 73
crossbars on 31, 32
direction 38
health indications 111
lines running from 30, 31
love and 76
marks on 30, 31, 51
missing 25, 30, 72
position 23, 28, 29, 31, 33, 41, 51, 57, 59, 64, 71, 73
splitting 51
time spans 39
wavy 29
Line of Travel 34-5, 41, 62-3, 118
Lines of Children 41, 66, 86-7
little finger see Finger of Mercury
liver 100, 102
Liver Line see Line of Mercury
longevity 6
love 6, 75-97
questions 96-7
sample reading 94-5

M

marriage 37, 40
material success 30-3

mathematicians 64, 65
megalomania 27
men's hands 39
  women's compatible with 83
mental problems 108-9
middle finger *see* Finger of Saturn
migraine 103, 112, 122
mimics 53
minor ailments 106-7
money 29-47, 82
motivation 22-3
Mount of Jupiter,
  developed 17, 26, 32, 46, 50, 52, 53, 55, 121
  flat 36, 50
  marks on 60, 77
Mount of Mars,
  colour 102-3
  developed 17, 26, 51, 63, 100, 121
  flat 100
  health indications 102-3
  marks on 102-3
  resilience 100
Mount of Mercury 33
  developed 17, 32, 33, 53, 56-7, 58, 59, 72
  health indications 102
  marks on 47, 65, 102
Mount of the Moon,
  colour 68
  developed 17, 37, 45, 51, 52, 59, 62-3, 66, 72, 77
  health indications 102, 103, 111
  Line of Fate rising from 28, 32, 37
  Line of the Sun rising from 33, 51, 52
  marks on 103
Mount of Saturn,
  developed 17, 22, 25, 31, 53, 58, 60, 64
  flat 17, 31, 32
  health indications 102, 110
  marks on 35, 102
Mount of the Sun,
  developed 17, 29, 31, 32, 50, 59, 67
  flat 31, 50
  health indications 102
  marks on 31, 46, 47, 102
Mount of Venus,

colour 81
developed 17, 31, 50, 51, 52, 62, 66, 77, 80, 81, 95
flat 17
Line of Fate rising from 36
Line of the Sun rising from 46
marks on 36-7, 84, 88
space on 77
Mounts, positions 17

N
nails 19, 101, 104-6
narrow hand 11
nervousness 102, 122

O
open hand 10, 11
orators 54-5
outdoor types 62-3

P
painters 50-1
palm,
  colour 100, 103
  dampness 101
  hollow 29, 77
  resilience 83, 100
  shape 82-3, 62
  texture 83, 90, 101
  'three worlds' 18
palmistry, method 6-7, 124
passion 80-1
performers 52-3
perspiration 122
pessimism 102
phalanges *see* fingers
philosophic hand 13, 25, 79, 107
photographers 72
pianist 72
Plain of Mars 37, 100
pointed fingers 14, 15, 79, 83
pointed hand 13, 24-5, 29, 107, 112
pointing 10
politicians 52, 53

possessiveness 81, 84
potential 49-73
potters 50, 73
pressure 112-13
priests 52, 53
psoriasis 106
psychic signs 68-9

Q
quadrangle 46, 67, 68-9, 72, 76, 123

R
rascettes 22, 123
recovery from illness 114-15
relationships 75-97
  questions 96-7
relaxation 116, 119, 123
religious leaders 53
reserve 81, 82
rheumatism 103
right hand 12
ring finger *see* Finger of the Sun
Ring of Solomon 68
rings,
  fingers worn on 10
  twisting 10

S
scientists 64-5, 72
sculptors 50-1
self-esteem 108
selfishness 81
sensuality 80
seven-year cycles 34, 38
shape of hands 13
Simian Line 39, 63, 81, 90-1, 95, 116-17, 123
sinusitis 103
'sister' lines 42, 92, 112, 115
sleep 107, 122
small hands 11
soft hands 55, 66, 83, 103, 108, 116
soft-skinned palms 83, 101
solitary activities 73
spatulate fingers 14, 51, 53, 56, 62, 79
spatulate hand 13, 24, 26,

31, 32, 53, 107
spontaneity 79, 82, 83
sportspeople 63
square fingers 14, 15, 58, 62, 78-9, 82
square hand 13, 24, 26, 31, 62, 78-9, 83, 107, 112
square palms 58, 82, 95
squares 30, 31, 77, 92, 103, 112, 115
stars 28, 103, 105, 112
stomach troubles 102
structural skills 58-9
success 28-33

T
tact 15
talent 49-73
tassels 111
teachers 60-1
tensions, necessary 116-17
three worlds of the hand 18
three-dimensional skills 58-9
throat problems 102
thumb,
  bump on pad 33
  flexibility 15, 26, 33, 60, 95
  length 15
  position held 10, 116
  shape 15, 26, 67, 116, 119
  weakness 36, 115
time factor 38-41
tolerance 67
trauma 112-13
travel 34-5
triangles 35, 47, 56, 60, 61, 69, 77, 103

V
'V' sign 10
varicose veins 102
violence 90

W
women's hands 39
  men's compatible with 83
writers 54-5, 70-1, 72
Writer's Fork 54-5, 71

AUTHOR'S ACKNOWLEDGEMENTS

I would like to thank all my friends for their enthusiasm, love and support over the years. I am especially grateful to Juliet Fishbourne, Tessa Strickland and Dinah Kibby, for having faith in my ability to write this book. Finally, to my mother, Josephine, for inspiring my initial interest in palmistry.

Eddison · Sadd Editions

Editor   Michele Doyle
Designer   Sarah Howerd
Design Assistant   Pritty Chauhan
Illustrators   Anthony Duke
                                Steve Pearse
                                Dave Sexton
Chapter-opener Illustrator   David Loftus
Proof-readers   Zoë Hughes
                                Sam Merrell
Indexer   Dorothy Frame
Production   Hazel Kirkman
                                Charles James